#Hustle4Ever

How to Write Your Own Definition of Success and **Win at Life.**

By Coach David Seay

Copyright © 2019 by David Seay

All rights reserved. No part of this book may be reproduced or used in any manner without written permission of the copyright owner except for the use of quotations in a book review. For more information, address: david@seaydevelopment.com

FIRST EDITION
First paperback edition November 2019

ISBN 978-1-7343539-1-4

Dear Self,

I like you

… and this time,

I mean it.

−Me

Who should read this book?

All Ages

All Genders

All Ethnicities

All Education Levels

All Socio-Economic Statuses

All Niches and Areas of Interests

All Income and Employment Levels

All Geographic Areas of All Countries

David Seay's Book, Hustle4Ever: How to Write Your Own Definition of Success and Win at Life, is an inspirational work that unveils David's life philosophy as a part of his exhortation for the reader to create their own "unique, authentic life success." The reader will have the ability to educate and motivate themselves to follow Coach Seay's lead in developing their own playbook to help live a complete and well rounded life.

This book combines a detailed breakdown of the different components of David's "Hustle4Ever" System with his life story – how to get where you want to get – and worksheets and other exercises and methods to help the reader create and implement their own version of success. All these elements add up to a deep and rich mix of ingredients that result in an executable strategy customized just for you.

Today is a time of information abundance that provides coaching, mentoring and dedicated personal growth planning for top achievers both online and offline through personal coaching sessions. Hustle4Ever is a book and resource that brings that process to life in one book that is for movers and shakers that don't necessarily need one on one coaching sessions, but are on the cusp of truly making an impact or need to hit the pause button and simply rebalance their growth perspective and strategies. We are not that far away from refining ourselves. We simply need a little help writing our own definition of success.

What is in this book?

You are.
Young people, adults and senior citizens alike, we all get one life experience.
I set people up for success and help people recognize their potential and convert it to actions and results. Powerful ideas, inspiring stories, strategies, tools and how to apply them are within the pages ahead. The lost get found here and the mediocre become great.

If you think, even for one minute, that you are living below your life's potential, or if you simply need a self-reset, this book is for you, no matter how old you are.
Let's Hustle to Win at Life.

ABOUT COACH SEAY

David Seay (Coach Seay) believes that we can all win at life and define our own success. With his "#Hustle4Ever" Way of Life, he leads, equips, and inspires others on the importance of living a well-rounded life and a life of intention, caring enough to pursue God's will for one's life, and how to positively impact others along the way. He provides the strategy for any age to find their own personalized strategic way of life.

A Christian, husband, father, son, brother, fitness enthusiast, entrepreneur, business owner, coach and volunteer, David has figured a few things out the hard way and has invested his time, talent and treasure to reduce the learning curve for you. He offers a clear path towards **REAL LEADERSHIP, GENUINE FULFILLMENT and FOCUSED LIVING** for a powerful life of continuous improvement, spiritual growth, personal development and real contribution, not simply in theory but in actual life application. Don't leave God's potential for your life on the table. Care enough about your own life to honor your journey on earth and embrace your inner underdog and grow into you the full vision God has for your life.

"There is no real success in just making it through this life. This life will end. It can be a tough lesson to embrace just like it was for me. You can impart a legacy to the next generation or not, the choice is yours. When you put something out there, you take a risk. When you keep something inside, you take a risk too. Put it out or keep it in, there's risk on both sides. I say put it out there and don't look back. God created your life to be unique for a reason. A Well-Rounded Life wins, so write your own definition of "Success"
and go Win at Life."
                              - Coach Seay

The Hack Pack™
You can find the "Hack Pack" a few ways to best compliment your personal learning style. You can download the guide for free as a part of your book purchase on our website. You will also find the Hack Pack mixed into the book at the key times when you need the right tool. This is a great way to capture momentum in the moment that you can refine later in the Action Section. You can also find the Hack Pack in the Action Section at the back of the book (not the end, this book does not end).

What Topics Are In This Book?

THE HUSTLE FACTOR

READ AND GET SPEED

THE #Hustle4Ever Way of Life

#Faith4Ever

#Family4Ever

#Fitness4Ever

#Business/CommUnity4Ever

#H4E TEACHABLE MOMENTS EXPLAINED

THE STORY OF HUSTLE

THE #Hustle4Ever Way of Life BREAKDOWN

THE RISE OF THE FAMILY

BUILD YOUR FAMILY PLAN

FAMILY OBJECTIVES

WHEN YOU STRIKE CONTRIBUTION GOLD

THE SIGNIFIGANCE MELTDOWN

BELIEF BLOCK

PLACE A PREMIUM ON ACTION

THE COMPARISON MODEL IS BROKEN

EXPERIENCE IS THE BEST TEACHER

ENDLESS SUMMER(S)

COMPLETING FAILURE(S)

MY LOVE STORY

SHORT, SWEET, AND TO THE POINT—THE ELEVATOR PITCH

WHO WRITES YOUR DEFINITION OF SUCCESS?

A BAG OF BALLOONS

YOUR SUCCESS BEGINS WITH A SUCCESSFUL THOUGHT LIFE

LOVE CONCEPT APPLIED- GOD HELP US BLESS EACH OTHER

POSITIVE AFFIRMATION STATION

A PREMIUM MUST BE PLACED ON ACTION POWER LIFT YOUR BRAIN

PEOPLE WATCHING STARTS IN THE MIRROR

IT AIN'T ABOUT ME...YET

JOY + LOVE = PEACE. BOOM! LOVE FINALLY EXPLAINED

LOVE CONCEPT APPLIED- GOD HELP US BLESS THE ELDERLY

SEASONS OF LIFE

DOES THIS BOOK EVER END?

THE RALLY

ABOUT COACH DAVID SEAY

THE 4EVER

ACTION SECTION

#Hustle4Ever TEACHABLE MOMENTS

    A Plan Begins With Reflection

    Critics, We Love You

    The 1% Rule

Show Up To Grow Up

Love Concept Applied- God Help Us Bless The Children

Participation Is Not Mandatory

Resource Overload

If You Want to "Be The Man"

Hey Ladies, If You Want To "Be Superwoman"

Young Adults See You

Remain Available To Help

Volunteer Like a Baller

The Acceptance Envelope

Quadruple Threat Position

Open Up To Affirmations

Suicidal Thinkers Take Action THE Teachable Moment

The Love Spectrum

Your Hard Pivot

THE HUSTLE FACTOR

Do you remember where you were the day you realized that one day, you will have to die? Shivers down the spine, I know… it's a lot to comprehend. While I'm much better now about how I feel when I think about my own mortality, that wasn't always the case. It took me quite a while to get past the fear and the questions of what this life experience is all about. I would be lying to you if I tried to tell you that sometimes the thought of our human mortality doesn't still bother me, but in the meantime, the clock is still ticking on **the one life that I have to live and I want nothing more than to achieve my full potential and be happy in the process, living out a successful, well-rounded life** and that is what I want for you as well.

I can't stand waste. I don't like to see resources wasted. From food to toilet paper, **waste is not cool—but a wasted life? That is the most uncool thought out there.** The world is inhabited with so many people with so much human potential, and you and I are one of "those" people. This book is your chance to finally realize your full, unique value and articulate what you are here for and how you are going to look back on your last day of life and know that you truly did your best and that you accomplished a life well lived.

The #Hustle4Ever Way of Life is my lifestyle choice. This is what works for me. Even if everything that I do doesn't resonate with you, I'm cool with that because the main take-away for you should be that **I have the ability to tell you what I am pursuing for the rest of my life** to make sure I **"ring the bell"** on the last day and you can bet I am sliding into my casket head first like the winning base runner rounding third.

Crazy—I actually have a plan and I can express it and when I say it, you can see people realize that they need the same thing. **YOU, ME, and WE need a bona fide plan in order to write our own definition of success and to be able to get on the path of accomplishing it.** That is all I want for you and all that each of us should ever want. Throughout this book, simply put, I am going to set you up for your own success, **REPEAT—YOUR OWN SUCCESS.** Not the success that someone else has, but yours. **Your UNIQUE, AUTHENTIC, LIFE SUCCESS** that you can embrace and be proud of. The success that is going to connect you to silly little words like Joy, Peace and Fulfillment that most folks simply don't understand and only see at shopping malls when Christmas rolls around. I am talking about **JOY, PEACE and FULFILLMENT** that is real and feels real! So let's start cooking with gas and get your life fired up.

HUSTLE.

Most people can appreciate hustle. Street smarts, grind factor, common sense, and good old-fashioned work ethic have generated millions and billions of dollars. Of course, there's no lack of academic-based hustle either. There is a tremendous amount of brainpower and strategic thinking in hustle. It's what I call **Quadruple Threat Position.** You can find hustle in sports, business, politics, churches, and even prisons (for ill-advised tactics of hustle, of course, but even folks that have been incarcerated can hustle back to the righteous path). We will focus on the positive action verb for hustle, just for clarification—you know what I mean, the "let's make it happen" kinda hustle. Blue collars and white collars alike cherish the concept of hustle. Hustle is timeless and constantly in vogue because it implies someone is making something BIG happen and it's going to be pretty cool and you will want to post, blog, tweet, like, or follow it. So I feel it is important that we begin by breaking down the art and science of hustle.

While we all love goals, sometimes we get lazy in the pursuit of them. We can't let our hustle be a stray arrow. Hustle is about urgency, and the clock is ticking on your life and mine so as much as we love the concept of hustle, we need to bear down on the actions of concentrated hustle… a real, focused effort on the pursuit of and, more importantly, the true execution of hustle. Boom! That's what I'm talking about right there… **when hustle turns into muscle.**

We live in a world full of noise, talk, and empty intentions. Actions most definitely speak louder than words, and it's time to place a premium on action. I am a real-life kind of coach, probably much like the person that you hope to become or even the person that you already are who simply needs some fine-tuning or a small dose of belief like I do at times. You won't find me in the hall of fame for the NBA or NFL. You won't find my name in the hall of fame at the college sports level either. I didn't retire from professional sports with a championship ring turned sportscaster or anything close to that, but you will find me in the hearts and minds of those that I have coached in both sports and life, some as a coach and others just by setting an example. Most of these people can be found in my sphere of influence or what I like to call "the world around me", which is most likely the people I have met and the people that I see with frequency. If I had to tell you where much of my impact has proven to be, that would be with the children that I have coached in youth sports and youth camps and also with their parents and siblings, however my greatest place of impact has been in the lives of my own wife and children. You see, when you invest yourself authentically in the development of a child, you can't help but win over a parent. What parent doesn't appreciate someone volunteering their time to help their son or daughter become better, whether in sports or in life? Talk about an investment of goodwill. The payoff for everyone is tremendous and has compounding effects on so many levels. **You have hero potential, but you have to be bold enough to flex it.** The world needs more heroes. Not the kind in tights with bulging muscles flipping over cars and bringing criminals to justice, but normal men and women in communities that simply have a love of a particular sport or activity who authentically care about helping young boys and girls learn how to become better people through the use of games, arts or education and this applies to young people, adults and even senior citizens. There are two ways to coach. You can check the box and fulfill the obligation because no one else would sign up, or you can pour rocket fuel on your soul and go all in and understand that it isn't about you and that service first really is a bigger blessing for you than you can even imagine. As a coach, I have learned more about myself than any player I have ever coached, but the more I invest in my players and even their parents, the more energy I build towards my own development and it just naturally builds new models of example based leadership that actually help you win at life and take others with you on the journey.

One of the hardest parts of having influence over young players year after year is finding that you can't coach the same kids season after season because there are usually more kids than there are coaches and you ultimately have to pick teams and divide players. This past basketball season, I found myself with fourteen boys when I really wanted to coach thirty boys. We all know thirty players on one team isn't practical so I had to just focus on my fourteen, but in the previous off season, we ran an amazing training program under the leadership of some of the most pure people I have ever met in Alexa and Steve Harnig. They were the spark plugs behind, "The Grind", a simple theme Alexa and I put together. I saw boys and girls grow in the fundamentals of the game of basketball. Right under our noses, we were building a culture to "Grind Now and Shine Later", which is essentially the age-old truth that hard work pays off. I spent a lot of nights in the gym with kids of all ages along with a large group of other volunteer coaches. As we worked, I always paid special attention to my son and daughter and their peer groups as I know some of the boys will end up with me during the season and some of the girls would end up being teammates to my daughter and eventually some of my players in future seasons. I saw tremendous growth in each of these boys and girls, but do you know the greatest moment of intensity I witnessed? When I would get close to them and encourage them, even with just a whisper. The dribbles got sharper, the cuts deeper, the zags harder and the effort just plain bigger. How can just a word of encouragement double down the effort? Common sense is not always common practice. There is a void of encouragement in our youth and it is not the responsibility of the youth to encourage themselves. Sadly, I feel there is a lack of encouragement in our adult community as well. Just because you are grown, doesn't mean, you can't still rock at life if someone can just spark you at the right moment.

READ and GET SPEED

The #Hustle4Ever Life focuses on Faith, Family, Fitness, and Business/CommUnity. It's my key to a fulfilling a well-rounded life that Leads, Equips, and Inspires, all while taking other people with me on the journey toward achieving their maximum potential. It is not only a roadmap for my own true definition of the word success, but it can work for **anyone who truly hopes to reach their own maximum potential in this life and can also make you a person that truly loves to see other people achieve their dreams too and yes, high fives never go outta style. Never.**

So now is the point when you decide whether you are going to dig into this book or put it back on the shelf. If you don't want to read this book, don't worry about me. I will be just fine because I didn't write it for the sales stats, gold stars, or fanfare, but if you are looking for a way to **finally discover your hope and future and see what BIG plans are really waiting on you,** then this book is going to FINALLY help you put it all together in a condensed and organized blueprint for life success and shatter the fallacy that we all have the same definition of success.

This is how we will get you to your own **#HUSTLE4EVER Way of Life, a life grounded in Faith, Family, Fitness and Business/CommUnity.**

So I call it the #Hustle4Ever Way of Life. That is what gets me fired up. That is phrase or hashtag that puts fire in my belly. If that term doesn't resonate with you, but you are ready to find your game face and your zeal for life, then you have my permission to change it and I have made it easy for you to do so. Go for it. Maybe just that small change is the ignition moment that you have been waiting for.

#Hustle4Ever

"Way of Life" by Coach Seay

_____ Way of Life by _____

My Current Theme is _____

Joy and Happiness is a daily pursuit, not a destination. Map out goals that you want to accomplish and then pursue them with reckless abandon, defining your own success. The comparison model is broken so don't even play that game, but enjoy the journey to get your best life. God has a plan and a purpose for you at each season of your life. Don't believe anything other than that. You reap what you sow. Reap well.

1) #FAITH4EVER

I made a decision a long time ago that I was going to take my faith life seriously. Just like anything worth having, it requires work so don't think you are going to push a button and you will have faith. I love my Christian identity, although it is not always an easy path, but I have also decided to respect and coexist peacefully and in an educated manner with all other faith beliefs so if you don't identify with Christianity, you can still benefit from reading this book. Faith has a bad reputation, but it's funny because faith doesn't mean Christian or non-Christian. Faith is faith. Faith means believing that all is going to work out for the best, even if the journey has some bumps in the road along the way. For me, faith does have God behind it. For some, I understand that there isn't a deity behind their belief and I make no judgment there—however I expect no judgment in return. Now, put some goals down. How do you aspire to live your best faith life? Not so sure how faith fits in yet? That's okay, put down something of faith or spirit that you want to learn more about. Remember, progress before perfection. Now dream big and fill it in:

#Faith4Ever
_____
_____
_____
_____

2) #FAMILY4EVER

A friend of mine named Dan Mortimer, who has transitioned from heavy-duty construction man to poet, told me years ago, "I invest my life in those that are going to cry at my funeral." That was like a strong smelling-salt portion of ammonia after a figurative punch in the nose of reality. You can typically count on one or two hands the people that will stand around your casket and literally weep for the loss of your life. Everybody may show up and you may pack a whole church or synagogue, but when the proceedings are over, the casket is moved, and the body is laid to rest, there will be maybe five to ten people who are going to cry for you and for the loss of your life. Reflect on how you treat those people. Are they getting your best? Are they feeling loved, honored and respected by you? Are they getting the bitter part of you or the better part of you? If your stomach is sour right now, fear not. You can start restoring the legacy of your family right now, literally as soon as you stop reading.

If you have come from a toxic or broken family yourself, that does not mean that your current family (whether a single parent home or a underperforming marital home) has to experience what you experienced. The family is the most likely and controllable place for you to love, lead and serve other living things. Stop hitting the snooze button on your family and create or restore a family legacy in your home. Whether divorced or not, today is the day to start anew. Now, put some goals down. How do you want your family life to look? Not so sure? That's okay, put something down in writing, even if you don't believe it can happen. Remember, progress before perfection. Now dream big with love and fill it in:

#*Family4Ever*
___
___
___
___

3) #FITNESS4EVER

According to the U.S. Centers for Disease Control, the number one cause of death and injury in older adults is falling and fall related injuries. Have you ever slipped or fallen? Every person has fallen at least once. It's pretty scary, even if you recover your balance and don't fall, there is a moment of fear. Imagine going all the way down…hard. In your prime, it may just be bumps, bruises or a broken bone or two, but as we get older, falls can be more catastrophic, but we are all so very "busy" and working out means that we would need more time that we just don't have. Fall risks aside, your body is growing or decaying. There is no middle ground and as you age, you can only hope to slow the process of aging by fighting against the process and without a fight you are more likely to find a wheelchair or walker in your future. Posture and strength aside… how about energy? Wouldn't you like to increase your chances for more energy and real sleep? How about a positive self-image and mental clarity? Your body was designed to move and I believe our bodies are temples. Not temples that we should worship in a mirror, but temples that we should honor and respect and seek to improve so we can give our very best to the world around us. Fitness and Health go hand in hand. What goes in and on our bodies should be considered as well. Fitness and eating habits are not a chore, but they can feel that way until your perspective shift occurs. It will no longer be a chore to love and nurture yourself. Now, put some goals down. How can you find your fit? What does health and wellness look like for you if you were reflecting on your results one year from today? Not sure how to start? That's okay, put down something of health that treats your body and mind like a temple of physical strength and bodily confidence. Remember, habits can change. Now dream big, love on your ideal body image and fill it in:

#*Fitness4Ever*
___
___
___
___

4) #BUSINESS/COMMUNITY4EVER

When you meet someone new, how early in the conversation does someone ask "What do you do?" That isn't me. I don't ask that question. I trust that it will come up at some point as our conversation evolves or hopefully our relationship evolves, but you know just as well as I do that "What do you do?" comes up a lot, early and often in conversations. Conversationalists will coach you that this question is a great way to strike an affinity and shape the conversation, but I think it makes a good case on both side of the fence that what we do is extremely important to how we feel about ourselves and how we identify ourselves. But who sets up this definition? We do. We define ourselves and we need to accept full responsibility for this reality. We have selected our jobs. We have selected the businesses we run. We are where we are in our work lives because of past decisions and past courses of action, whether favorable or not. We wrap our identity up into our work. There is nothing wrong with this, unless you don't feel like you are doing something you love or don't see the greater good in your work. How about when we leave our life's season of work and move into retirement and our "golden years"? Here is where "the slash" comes into play. The slash between Business and CommUnity (#Business/CommUnity) represents the moment of "crossover" some would refer to their retirement life, but we are going to master the concept of not waiting to give back. Waiting doesn't help you and it certainly doesn't help the people that need you now. People need you now! Now, put some goals down. How can you be a great steward of your CommUnity? Not so sure what to do? That's okay, put down some organization or some person that you desire to help. You also have permission to be ambitious at work or in your business too. Remember, no dream… no drive. Now dream big, get ready to bless someone and fill it in:

#Business/CommUnity4Ever

_____
_____
_____
_____

FACT: The clock is ticking on your days to live on this planet, so put down the anchor, finally discern your true worth, and grow like a real hustler.

Now since we are all on our own journeys and on our own timelines of growth and development, you may be ready to wrap this up, move straight to your "Definition of Success" below and get out there and get after it. If you do, then get moving. Don't waste another minute. Write your definition of success and go crush it! If you need more time and want to keep moving, then put some notes or initial thoughts on your definition below and let's keep refining you as we go through the book. **You will get another chance to sharpen your words in the Action Section.**

My Definition of Success is:

_____
_____
_____
_____

Excellent! We are off to a great start, let's keep hustling. Let me tell you some more strategies and share my story with you.

"HUSTLE4EVER (#H4E) TEACHABLE MOMENTS" EXPLAINED

Kids love to scrimmage. Children just flat out love to play. The last thing they really want a coach to do is to stop the scrimmage and instruct and educate. Think about that. You don't know what you don't know (ignorance) until you know it (enlightenment), so if you only want to learn by your own mistakes (stubborn), then I won't come to practice anymore. Here is the ball (free will), have at it (reality). Let me know how it works out for you. The older kids get, the more they appreciate "Teachable Moments". This is what I say when I stop practice in order to instruct. It seems that if I say "Ok guys, Teachable Moment", they open up to receive the information better. Some receive the instruction better than others. Some simply roll their eyes. It's time for us to get this season of life underway for you, but in order to do that, we are going to have to get ready in the pre-season now. We are going to start working through installing the #Hustle4Ever Way of Life, so expect a few "Teachable Moments" along the way and let's get started.

#H4E Teachable Moment - A PLAN BEGINS WITH REFLECTION

The problem with plans is that many of us don't have one. And for those of us who do have a plan, we likely don't execute that plan well on a daily basis. It can be tempting to place too much emphasis on work or even our own selfish desires rather than reflecting inwardly and fairly accessing the value and purpose of our lives.

For years, I wrote and rewrote goals. I would make the New Year's resolutions. I had paper and electronic planners. Having a general sense of direction is certainly a good start, but **razor-sharp focus helps us find a new definition for success. When was the last time you studied your own definition of success?** We hear that word so often that we don't really understand what it means. Money can be a part of it. Promotions at work too. A happy family and the gift of health can fit in for sure. **Whether we believe it or not, the definition of success is a case-by-case, life-by-life definition.**

There are so many examples of perceived "success" out there, that it is difficult to accept even the dictionary definition of the word (more later on this). The truth of the matter is that we get the opportunity to write the story of our success each and every day. <u>**For me, success is living a well-rounded life where I use my time, talent, and treasure to live out God's unique purposes for my life, even though I can't see every step in the road and some gifts are still being opened.**</u> It has taken a long time to sharpen my focus, but now, it guides me on a path of life that will help me not only be joyful and at peace, but live in a way that allows me to say that I poured out all my potential, while it was my turn to live on earth. **It's the Hustler's Way of Life.**

THE STORY OF MY HUSTLE

I grew up in Charleston, South Carolina. Living a few places within the region, I attended public schools and probably wasn't the most popular kid in the traditional sense (we will discuss popularity later), but I certainly didn't have a lack of friends or self-esteem. I was the "friendly athlete" if you had to label me, and we all know that labels are a reality. I played many sports growing up as a child, but around twelve years old, I focused my efforts entirely on basketball, mainly just because my sister played and I wanted to beat her in the driveway one-on-one game. She was a good athlete, so it took a while to start beating her, but once I did, something ignited inside of me. Basketball became my life. Camps, drills, practice and pick-up games. I almost felt naked if I wasn't holding a basketball. I wanted to go places with basketball. The goal setting began.

Maybe the NBA. Certainly I would get a college scholarship, but I had to start with my first season of organized basketball.

I still remember my coach's opening address at my first ever team practice. "My name is (I have forgotten his name), and I look forward to coaching you this season. I didn't play college basketball, but I did play for my local high school." I was so disappointed. Weren't all recreational coaches former NBA and college legends? What was this high school wash-up going to teach me? Not much, I figured.

I don't remember much about him at all, but I do remember that season because it was a middle school reality check. I had no game. I wasn't the best on my team and wasn't even close to being the best in my league. I remember seeing other kids playing well and my stomach feeling queasy. I had some work to do. I started playing a lot of pick-up basketball in my neighborhood and would play well into the night in the driveway. Our driveway was sloped, so a jump shot could be eight feet high on one side and thirteen feet on the other, but it was cool anyway. Half the time, the spotlight wouldn't even put out enough light to illuminate the hoop, but I played anyway. My mom and dad weren't hoopsters themselves, but they were certainly supportive and let me have all the time I wanted in the driveway.

One weekend, my dad brought out the ladder on a Saturday while I was shooting. He had some weird-looking contraption in his hand, and he started removing the floodlight on the corner of the house. I watched curiously while I dribbled. I didn't have any fear that my dad was taking the light away. I am grateful I never felt like my parents wanted to punish more than set me up for success. Discipline is an art, and my parents were Picassos. I know a lot of kids can't say that, so I am grateful, but even as I write this, I know I still need to improve that type of spirit with my own children and I will accomplish it. My dad said from the ladder, "Dave, we are working on an upgrade here." I wasn't sure what he meant, but I figured it out when the sun went down because that night the switch was flipped in more ways than one. My dad had installed a commercial-grade halogen light the size of today's iPad Mini. It not only lit up our driveway but a few neighbors' houses as well. From then on, the driveway logged more games of "H-O-R-S-E" three-on-three, one-on-one, and free throw practice than you can imagine. That light saw multiple hoops replaced and dozens of nets. There was always some sort of game being played in the driveway.

I remember the day that some kids in the neighborhood told me that there was no way that I was going to make the local high school team. While the light being installed was the moment of ignition, this comment of doubt was like rocket fuel poured onto a fire, and the fire was in my belly. If you thought the driveway had been a busy place up to that point, it just got a whole lot busier.

#H4E TEACHABLE MOMENT – Critics, we love you.

Critics are real and you should take a moment to thank them, even if quietly in your hearts. Sounds funny, but I am not joking. The first time you experience a critic, you will be highly uncomfortable, especially if you have been fortunate enough to grow up with a support network. **Critics can help you examine yourself, which seems to be a lost art these days. Self-awareness, reflection, and self-examination are the keys to all forms of growth. Critics may have been in your house as you grew up and maybe even your parents.**

Mama said this, Daddy said that. What did they say? Did they unknowingly transfer their own insecurities down the family tree to you? Don't accept it. Regrets happen…failures happen. Tell shame to step off.

There were many phenomenal athletes walking the halls of Wando High School, and the basketball team was no exception. I started to pay much more attention to the teams and the talent level, and the training began in earnest. I remember discovering weight lifting, strength training, agility drills, and, most importantly, the value of dribbling drills. My mother used to come out in the garage to time me in select "Gus Macker" ball-handling drills. At first they were painful, but over time, dribbling became second nature. Left-handed dribble drills (I was right-handed), Mikan Drills, jump rope, and dot drills—it was the summer of hustle, and it continued day after day, week after week, month after month.

From middle school to high school, the work ethic and dedication to self-development never let up, and I ultimately found myself making the junior varsity team in middle school where I grew into the captain of the team the following year. A few years later, I was on the varsity team playing with some of the best talent in our area with the respect of my coaches, teammates, classmates, and even coaches from the opposing teams we played. I wrote the last two sentences in a matter of seconds, but they encapsulate a summary of a critical time in my life when **fundamentally sound character traits were being forged inside of my soul that still exist in my life today.** Two sentences can never describe all the steps, pains, injuries, self-doubts, and hours that poured into the development of the person I have become today and the aspiring vision of the person I am constantly hoping to become. **Personal paradigm shifts may only seem like small moments of maturity to the outside observer, but they truly are like tectonic plates moving inside your soul.**

No matter how many drills you do or how much you train, at some point, you have to put it into action, and if you don't apply the drills to a game situation, what was the purpose of the drills in the first place? Yes, drills and practice are the proving ground. **First when you prove it to yourself, then when you prove it to others.** So what is the purpose of drills? Duh, to get better, but in what way? Is it to have better overall reflexes or to install that one move into your game so it runs more smoothly next time?

#H4E TEACHABLE MOMENT –The 1% Rule

If you want to change by 100 percent, the easiest way to change is 1 percent at a time. As much as any athlete wants to incorporate a new skill into any game, it won't happen in one single day, most likely. Of course, there are rare cases of the genius who can pick things up on the first try, but for the large majority of us, **we need to be willing to invest in ourselves if we are ever going to grow.** From basketball training to corporate experience, self and professional development is readily available and **a choice.** Focus on the actual actions that will make you better. Intentions without action are lifeless. **You know just as well as I do that talk is cheap and actions speak louder than words, so take action.**

No one will ever force you to grow. Yesterday, I realized while I was driving that I enjoy learning so much more now than when I was a child. Today, I love to read and listen to books. When I was young, I would avoid summer reading like the plague. If I could roll back the clock and get the opportunity to read and learn when my brain was more receptive to learning as a young person, I would have read with more focus, incorporated more languages, and truly maximized the opportunity to learn and thrive in school. We often overlook the opportunities for improvement because they are so simple and typically right underneath our noses. It takes less than twenty seconds to make your bed each morning. There are many other things we can improve on a daily basis. The only reason we can't improve certain areas of our lives is because we **choose** not to. **Unfortunately, "can't" is a choice too.**

Belief is critical. As much as work ethic was revealed to me as a way to realize my dreams, there will always be outside, external influences that work for you or against you. Sometimes the forces simply keep you at rest, sitting in the same unproductive state that you have been in. This state of doing nothing is easy to maintain but hard to break. Sitting on the couch requires much less effort than exercising. It's hard to believe that even if you don't feel like exercising, once you actually start the good habit of working out, it gets easier to do each day and before you know it, you have a new good habit that has way more benefits for your life than you can even imagine. It is so important that we never forget that our mind is a muscle and we have the ability to control our thinking and build our beliefs. It was belief alone that started my self-improvement journey.

Mr. Otto German wasn't my head coach, but he made an impression on me. Coach German coached because he loved basketball, he loved his own children and wanted them to be successful, and he cared about the development of other children as well. Oh, and he was a volunteer coach too. It wasn't until years later that I discovered that he had also been an amazing basketball player for the College of Charleston.

I first met Coach German when I was playing in the recreational leagues in the Town of Mount Pleasant. The first time I met him was at an all-star practice. I don't really know how I ended up on that team because I remember not feeling *worthy* to be there (which is a whole other book LOL) once I saw all the talent that was on the team. The team consisted of all the leading scorers from the regular season. I don't remember scoring a lot during the season, but I had just had my growth spirt, so I am sure that must have had something to do with it. I felt out of place at all-star practice.

I can't even remember the other coaches, but I remember Coach German. Even as a child, I could tell he was fully invested every time he showed up to coach. Wearing a suit, or in a sweat suit (garnet velour, of course), he was pushing us and telling us the secrets of the game. He wasn't there just to coach kids, he was there to develop kids. His voice elevated to a different level when he was coaching.

When it was your turn to go in a drill, you wanted to impress him. You wanted to show him you had listened to the instructions and if you did something wrong in the drill when it was your turn, you were okay with him stopping the drill in front of all your friends because he was going to show you the right way… in a way… that it made sense. When you ran the drill the next time and actually got it right, he would celebrate you. That felt good. That was something to build on. That was when I started to understand what good energy looked like and started to appreciate getting "fired up." **Playing up in sports and in life—it's just cool.**

The rest of that all-star season was pretty lackluster in regard to our performance as a team. We played some pretty tough teams from other areas around Charleston that are still notorious for amazing youth basketball teams to this very day. I didn't get a lot of playing time. I can't fault any coach for that because I remember the fear when I got on the court, and I am sure it showed. **Fear is the kiss of death** on the basketball court, and you can't hide it for long. Even the environment was intimidating. It was a great learning experience, but even at my age, I knew there was work to do. I was up for it, however, because the flame of passion was burning in my heart. **I knew I could compete. I was ready to get out of my own way.**

I started attending summer basketball camps. College of Charleston was under the helm of Coach John Kress at the time. His camps were for boys of all ages up to rising high school seniors. People came from all over the state and beyond to go to the camp. The talent was impressive. I attended each summer. The first few years of camp, I was lost in the crowd, but I appreciated the drills and fundamentals the coaches taught at the camp.

There was something intriguing to me about working on technique, especially on defense. I realized defense was a place I could differentiate myself and where hustle paid off with a greater return on investment. I could hear Coach German in my head saying, **"Good defense generates easy offense."** I still tell my son, daughter and their teammates that today, but only because it is true. When you hustle, coaches start to pay attention. Even if you don't have all the natural talent in the world, you can earn almost anyone's respect with hustle. Plenty of people that played against me at camp might have been better, but they had to work harder when they played against me. **They were going to get boxed out. They were going to feel contact.** There weren't any freebies. I wasn't a dirty player by any stretch of the imagination, but I understood positioning and technique. I was a coach on the court. I didn't have to say anything either. The more textbook I could run a drill, the better. Disappointing a coach…that was pain beyond belief. In addition to the College of Charleston camp, I looked for any camp around town to try so I could improve—small church camps, recreation department camps, you name it. I met Coach Terry Lee at the Wando High School Youth Camp.

Coach Lee was a history teacher at Wando High School. I went to the camp with a friend who was also interested in playing junior varsity. While the camp had a lot of younger kids, I remember going home each night feeling like I had played well. I literally still remember one specific bounce pass I made that I know was the attention grabbing play that caught Coach Lee's eye. **It's funny how specific plays go onto our mental highlight reel for the rest of our lives.** That was my rising eighth-grade summer. All summer I had played hoops and school was just about to start in August. I would be finishing my last year in middle school and had heard about the Wando Junior Varsity tryouts. It was the longest school year from August to late September… waiting for the basketball season to begin. My eighth-grade math teacher was the JV Coach, so I knew tryouts were coming soon as he announced it in class. There were dozens of eighth-grade boys who wanted those junior varsity positions, but only two were available. The day of tryouts finally came. I wish I could remember all the details, but I do remember how intimidating it felt to see over four hundred boys vying for two positions. Maybe it wasn't four hundred, but it sure felt like it was. I was fortunate to make the team along with a classmate.

#H4E TEACHABLE MOMENT – Show up to grow up

I am always shocked to see how many times kids want to stay home when big events come along. This past season, an older boy I know didn't go to JV tryouts. I am not sure how much he loved the game of basketball, but I would have put a pretty good probability on him making the team due to the tremendous height he had and how he is projected to get even taller in the next season. Just the sheer fact that so many kids wanted only a few positions kept him from going to tryouts. I have been cut before. It hurts, but to not show up… I don't feel like that sets you up for the chance to see how you measure up. I can only remember a few times in my life that I regret going somewhere. Most of the time, I grow when I show. Put your head out of the shell from time to time and see what is going on. Be proud of who you are and see what opportunities come your way.

#H4E TEACHABLE MOMENT
LOVE APPLIED - GOD HELP US BLESS THE CHILDREN

From priests that have molested altar servers to trusted coaches that have betrayed parents by sabotaging children to Mr. Huxstable peddling pudding pops, adults are going to fail children. Knowing this does not make it acceptable. Adults are not being rude when they ask tough questions of coaches and chaperones. If a volunteer at school is too lazy to complete a background check then they need not chaperone or be on campus, and if the school is too lazy to validate a volunteer's status, no matter how many donations they have made, then a parent should speak up and not be afraid to hold the school accountable or remove administrators. If a priest can molest a child (even as a Catholic myself), then as much as I hate to say it, anything (and any sin) is possible. Great sins have grown from simple thoughts of impurity. Unfortunately, not everyone has the ability to guard their mind, so we need to guard what we can. Children don't think like we think and they shouldn't have too, but because of adults, they have to. A young person will give an adult the benefit of the doubt until they are old enough not to or until they have a reason not to. Children don't even use certain portions of their brains that are necessary to critical thinking until much later in their development.

Halfway through my eighth grade JV season, our head coach didn't show up to practice. About ten minutes after practice was scheduled to start, Coach Lee and Coach German arrived. They informed us that our junior varsity head coach would no longer be coaching and that going forward Coach German and Coach Lee would share the coaching duties. Talk about an opportunity walking in the door. It was always nice to see Coach Lee and Coach German regardless, but the reason for their taking the helm was unsettling. It turned out our previous coach had been arrested for sexual misconduct with minors. We watched him being taken off by the police in handcuffs that night on the evening news. I never saw that coach again, but Coach German and Coach Lee taking over was the biggest blessing I could have asked for. How can the coach you have shape your life? It doesn't seem reasonable to believe that a coach can have that much of an impact, but trust me... **it matters. Remember this and PLEASE HONOR IT.**

I seriously wanted to impress Coach Lee and Coach German. The best part was that they recognized the effort I was putting in, much of which happened during the off-season. Outside of our regular season, I trained in our gym and weight room as much as possible. I lived close enough to ride my bike to the school and if the gym was open and the courts were free, **or if I even suspected the gym was open,** I would head over. If the weight room was unlocked, I was in there. I wasn't all that muscular, but over time, I surprised myself with my strength. I formed my own club, the "SBS Crew" which stood for "Skinny But Strong". Other coaches from other sports would try to recruit me to play their sports. I did end up playing baseball a few off-seasons simply because the coach asked me every other day to come out and give it a try. He saw me workout in the weight room with his baseball team while I was in the basketball off-season. He appreciated my work ethic. He appreciated my dedication. I would even venture to say, he appreciated my hustle.

Evidently, hustle is in demand, and I am more than happy to accept that as a competitive advantage in sports and in life. The football coach even tried to recruit me, but by that time, I was too in love with basketball and my game was making strides toward the varsity level. So how do you sharpen your focus and **WRITE YOUR OWN DEFINITION OF SUCCESS**? Here is the way to **WIN AT LIFE:**

THE #HUSTLE4EVER WAY of LIFE BREAKDOWN

I live a #Hustle4Ever Lifestyle... it's my way of life. It took me years to get there. It took time, effort, and money to discover it, but I wouldn't change anything on the journey because **I have decided to embrace learning from the positive and the negative**—although I like the positive experiences much better. It even took me time to come up with a name for this way of life, but now that I have put a title on it, #Hustle4Ever, I can hold myself accountable and also articulate it and transfer it to my family legacy and to the "world around me".. (also known as the people we encounter most frequently).

It may sound absolutely absurd and even corny to have a name for a way of life, but labels define us. If you don't believe me just look around. Brand names matter to us. We promote brands all day, every day, mostly subconsciously, (some of which we probably wouldn't even support if we took the time to understand what they were all about), so let me tell you about my way of life and then I will help you create yours. The #Hustle4Ever Lifestyle focuses on these four principles:

1. FAITH
2. FAMILY
3. FITNESS
4. BUSINESS/COMMUNITY

Period. End of story. It is that easy. Here it is again:

The #Hustle4Ever Way of Life:

1. FAITH – #Faith4Ever
2. FAMILY - #Family4Ever
3. FITNESS - #Fitness4Ever
4. BUSINESS/COMMUNITY - #Business/CommUnity4Ever

So simple... so clean. It rolls off the tongue. This works for me, and I believe it can work for you too. I am going to tell you what it all means, but if you don't like everything I say, word for word, then I will guide you through how to develop your own way-of-life label of real empowerment. So let's work on the fundamentals together because it's the fundamentals that matter.

1. #FAITH4EVER

So how do you build a positive faith life? You have to practice one and you have to want faith and candidly, you typically have to put in work to obtain faith. It shouldn't feel like work, but sometimes it does because we can struggle to understand love and joy. "Joy" sounds like a lame word only because it is not easily found and certainly misunderstood. **Joy is a daily choice and a journey... both at the same time. As much as joy is actually an emotion and defined as a "feeling", it is really not a feeling at all, it is a fact and here is the truth behind it. God loves you and God loves me.** He loves us both more than we can even imagine and it is extremely difficult to express this reality, but let me try. If you are a good parent, it is going to be easier for you to understand this, but even if you aren't a parent, I think you can understand it as well. One night, I tucked my kids into bed. That particular night, I had struggled in my relationship with my son and while I can't remember what we were fighting about, I just know that we fought that day and it was a hard day for our relationship. We reconciled just before I turned his lights out and as much as I was irritated with him, I was just as much in love with him and I knew that our relationship had unconditional love. I peeked in on my other children as I headed back to my room where my wife was already asleep. When I turned out the lights and put my head down on the pillow for the night, I reflected on how I could have lived better that day. I like to replay the day in my mind and think about my own behavior. I asked for forgiveness of my sins and failings and it occurred to me that I was reliving the "tucking in" I had just had with my own children moments ago. God loved me despite my sins. God wanted me to know he loved me in that moment unconditionally. I had peace accepting forgiveness and God's unconditional love and then I slept and thankfully the next day, I had another chance with myself and with my son. Truly allowing your faith to guide your life is a challenge because we are all human. Fear not, party people! Faith is always available, and a happy life begins on the inside first. **No one knows your thoughts and desires better than you.** Without joy or the pursuit of joy, you risk allowing external forces to shape your definition of success and happiness and **open yourself up to comparison.** And that game is broken. **Faith is not and cannot only be a feeling and life begins with love. Faith is about being okay loving yourself second and allowing God to love you first. If you don't believe that there is a God that loves you,** I will respect your decision, but I will maintain my opinion that God loves you. We hear about the cup running over, but the cup can't run over if you have a lid on your own cup of faith first. Let the Lord show you his purposes for your life and experience true fulfillment and that is when you will finally have a sense of peace and therefore become a blessing to the world around you. I will be the first one to tell you that sometimes you will "feel it" in your faith and other times you might not, but the practice of faith can be just as important as the actualization of faith. We spend months planning the start of a business and we spend years studying academics in school, but we try to simply listen at church for an hour a week and hope that we will have some vision from God to show us how we are going to get on the right path and live out the most fulfilling life ever. A faith life is the keystone to a successful life. I used to think a keystone was just added for flair, but a keystone is essentially the anchor stone at the summit of an arch that ties everything together. If the keystone wasn't present, the whole arch would crumble. Someone figured this out a long time ago and now we intentionally put the keystone in the arch. Your faith life has to be intentional. It can be simple, but it has to have some daily action. For me, I like daily and weekly faith goals. Daily prayer is important to me. Daily spiritual reading is just as important to me as well. My process doesn't have to be your process, but here is my process:

1) I wake up and express sincere gratitude to God for all that he has given me including my new day of life, my health, my wife, my choice to grow and my family. I thank him for many other things as well, but I "sit" in the gratitude and let him know that I am truly thankful. As corny as it might sound, when my first foot hits the floor in the morning, I say "THANK" when the first foot hits and "YOU" when the second foot greets the day.

2) I visualize success and believe God wants good things for me. I carry my affirmations with my during my day and use them to grow and reinforce my beliefs.

3) I pray my rosary daily. This was a hard thing to get started, but I have now been doing it for years and I have experienced a different level of wisdom and reflection by doing this each morning. You don't have to pray the rosary to have the same experience. Opening each day in quiet prayer can work as well. I will just say my most significant actions in my life were spoken to me were found quietly during my rosary time.

4) I read the scripture of the day. I literally get an email early in the morning so it is on my phone for me to read. The way my Catholic Faith is set up, our entire church reads the same readings and gospel around the world on the same day and if you

read it every day for three years, you will have read the entire Bible. It is so easy to invest five minutes or less a day to read the Bible rather than trying to read the entire book cover to cover in large sittings. This daily process has helped me build a large base of understanding of God's word and all of the stories of the Bible so I cannot only support my thought process in life, but also deepen my understanding of faith and it never fails that I hear the right reading on the right day when I need it most. Now, you can even listen to the readings on a podcast channel each day. USCCB (United States Council of Catholic Bishops) is the podcast and website I use.

5) I attend a weekly group to study and discuss my faith with other people. Once per week, I meet with a men's group that I helped organize a few years ago. I joke with the guys that I just set the group up so I could have free therapy. It's a half joke-half truth. Too often, we try to figure it all out on our own. We let pride get in the way of progress and getting answers. The group is simple, yet effective and anyone can start a group. We open each meeting in prayer, read the gospel for that day and then have a very small reflection on the reading and within minutes, a natural discussion takes over. We have guys in the group ranging from their twenties to their eighties. Sometimes our priest will even come. The group has good energy and is like an episode of "Everybody Loves Raymond" most of the time. Very relaxed and real, yet so comfortable for so many. We have many other groups at our church as well. Some are for men and some for women and some are for both. "Grouping" on some level is important. It helps keep you connected and can help you in both good and bad times. Fellowship with others on the same journey of life as you just makes life easier.

6) I attend church each Sunday and fulfill the Holy Days of my faith and make sure my wife and children do the same. God has been very good to me. Not to say that he has just dropped everything I want in my lap, but God has helped me in so many areas of my life. I attend church each week as my simple way to say thank you. It took me years to understand that I didn't need to "get something" out of going to church. For years, I walked out of church saying, "I wish the sermon would have been more applicable to me" or "I don't feel like my heart was in that service". Man, was I missing the point. **The day I realized that going to church was all about worship, my whole life changed.** Church is my time to let God fully know how grateful I am for His existence and His eye over my life. I have enough and I am grateful. We always say to "count our blessings", but we can easily convince ourselves to complain about the blessings we wish we had. If we don't appreciate the blessings we hold in our hands today (even if only a few), you can bet you are keeping any other blessings from coming your way. If you have ever heard about the glass being half empty (pessimistic point of view) or half full (optimistic point of view), you can appreciate that God has provided to each of us a chalice to hold. He doesn't want to give us a half full or half empty view of abundance, he wants to run the cup over with blessings so that the overflow goes to those we have the power to bless around us. The more we stay stuck on half empty or half full, the less we will really have a cup that overflows. Changing my church experience to worship mode did this for me. It can happen for you too. Flip to gratitude and watch the blessings flow.

#H4E TEACHABLE MOMENT – Participating is not mandatory

In church, we tend to act like zombies. We say the same prayers and do the same motions each week. While the church calendar is alive and the messages and readings are different at every service, church can feel the same. Guess who is in control of that? Yep, you are. Challenge yourself to know every word of the service by heart and FULLY participate in the service. Instead of looking down and reading words, speak them with passion and meditate on the cross or an impactful image or statue in your church. Let your passion and vigor for participation set a righteous example for the future generations of your family. Read the readings and scriptures before you arrive at church. Show up with a desire not to miss one single moment of worship. Drip on every word and let your soul be alive for one hour. Church isn't about you, it is about worship so worship and see how your spiritual life changes. You will never be the same. You will know God. You will be a light to the world around you.

There are many more things I can do to deepen my faith and grow my own personal relationship with God the Father and Jesus Christ. I am engaged in my faith because I have invested in my faith so now I am more aware of the opportunities to grow and serve and more growth is planned in the future because **I have made growth intentional** so now it is a part of my walk. There are opportunities all around you to grow your faith. Retreats, small groups, service opportunities, leadership opportunities, even business related needs if that is your thing. The important thing to do is to get involved and find a place to fit in. We all fit in somewhere so don't get discouraged if that fit seems elusive. It simply takes time sometimes to find it, but it is there if you will keep looking. You have to expect to actually find it one day. We can't seek and NOT expect to find it. Seek and EXPECT to find your spiritual connection and trust me, it will happen.

Yes, religion is personal and can polarize and alienate if you try to shove it down another person's throat, but I make no apology for believing in God. Yes, I believe in Jesus. Again, no apology. I appreciate my religious freedom in the United States and for those who fight to protect all freedoms and rights. **I do not condemn other faiths, <u>and I do not want to go to war with people who might not share my religious beliefs.</u>** At the same time, however, I have no problem sharing my faith and my journey with God and explaining how **I believe God can unify everything under the sun and <u>I believe that He will and that we will look back together as a people and see all the chances we missed to have a deeper understanding of one another.</u>** I am always curious about other faiths and respect their practices, especially the Jewish faith. I read the Old Testament as well as the New.

Since I believe in Jesus Christ, it is my goal to strive to emulate him or as much as we know about his earthly life. I read the Bible daily to stay connected with the character of God and of Jesus **so that I can use that information for my spiritual and practical growth in this life.** If you know anything about Jesus, he was steady. He often surprised people by how he would respond to difficult questions and scenarios with dignity, grace, and proper communication. I believe many of our issues and conflicts could go away if we had this type of approach. Steven

Covey captivated me with the "Seek First to Understand" Principle in The Seven Habits of Highly Effective People. **Staying "in the pocket" during conflict resolutions can be a hard task to accomplish, but working at communication—whether it is with your spouse, your child, your employer, your employees, or even a religious radical—can make a lot of problems go away.** A spirit of faith in your life can help you live your life with a sense of love and abundance that all people were created equal and their lives have value. **When we choose to see the value in other people, even when we have to dig well below the surface, we allow doors to open and bridges to be built.** Since I am expressive of my faith, I often have people ask me about faith. All I can say is that I encourage you to take a spiritual journey with yourself. Don't wait to "get around to it". You are missing a taste of daily joy and peace by waiting. The journey starts with the first step and yes, the Bible is applicable today and very practical if you spend the time to read and seek to understand it. Scripture can always help in any situation. The more you know, the better.

Here is an opportunity to capture some thoughts related to this section:

#Faith4Ever:
_____
_____
_____
_____

2. #FAMILY4EVER

We all know that each family has a past and it has a future. Now, I can't do anything about the past of my family, but I can certainly do something about my present and my future. Of course, the present is probably on the top of my mind, but the future is really only up to me. **Legacies are real. Family legacies are even more real and lazy doesn't equal legacy. It takes effort.**

The behaviors we see today in our families are essentially learned behaviors from the people who raised us. **That is our typical baseline of human behavior,** which we have no control over for many years. As much as our individual life experiences have helped shape us, the culture of our family (or lack of family) in the past wants to dominate our household and relational behavior. **That can be good and bad.** If you come from a wonderful family, where your mother and father were happily married for your entire childhood, you are going to have a different concept of family than the mom or dad who was raised in a home where the parents were divorced due to drug abuse and experienced constant violence in the home. Now those might be two very extreme examples, but we all know people who have come from both of these scenarios and we can see that they have different concepts of family. **There is no judgment here for the person who comes from a tough upbringing.** There are people growing up at this very moment in tough situations as well. In reality, we have **humans raising humans,** and we can all agree that no one is perfect.

Regardless of your concept of family, you can write your own family legacy. You MUST write your own family legacy. Good traditions and examples of behavior need to be passed down, while poor behaviors or negative experiences need to be removed and eliminated. **It is my hope that there is a strong father leading your household.** Today, you will hear again and again that there is a male leadership problem in America. Could this be true? Children and wives alike appreciate strong fathers. **A strong father is one who loves his wife and honors her. He makes it obvious to the children that he still loves his wife and that he expects the children to respect the mother because he also respects the mother.** I have been blessed to know many strong women in my life. Women with leadership qualities, women who are successful in their careers and can still balance home life with grace. I have seen wonderful stay-at-home moms that contribute and volunteer at school as well. I am working on raising strong women. **All that said, I have yet to find a strong woman that had any objection being led by a man as long as that man was a good leader as a husband and a father.** In my experience, even the strongest and most successful women enjoy a man leading well in the home, **IF THE MAN DESERVES TO BE THE LEADER.** While guys won't want to hear this, all issues in a marriage or family can be traced back the father or husband's leadership. **A woman needs to know that the man is fully invested in the success of the family, and she certainly doesn't want to feel like she is doing it all on her own.** We all know that there are extreme examples on both sides of the equation. We have all heard of the mother that was unfaithful to the father and the father that was unfaithful to the mother. Those are lose-lose situations regardless of how the issue got started, but chances are that they started with a man who was tuned out from his wife's and family's needs.

Self-justification has led many people away from being a solid family.

I will be the first to admit that running a family and a household is not an easy job, but families stand the test of time when they stick together. I was very fortunate to have heard the following statement from my friend Dan Mortimer early in the creation of my family. I mentioned it earlier, but it deserves repeating. **He said, "I invest my life in those people that are going to cry at my funeral."** That comment was a stark reality check, and I use that test to this day. Of course we would like to think that on the day of our funeral, a national holiday is going to be established and the flag will be lowered to half mast in our honor, but the reality is that while many will likely show up and pay their respects, your most loving relationships that will tremendously miss you after your passing can be counted on less than ten fingers and maybe two toes at the most. We have to keep our priorities in order and dedicate our lives to developing and protecting families. In the last few years, I have found great clarity in looking at a visual of the Holy Family. Regardless of your faith choice, families can appreciate the model of The Holy Family. **What good is it for a father to be a champ at the office and a chump at home?** Men, don't give your family leftovers at home. Come home with just as much gratitude as exhaustion from work. Both are a blessing.

Here is an opportunity to capture some thoughts related to this section:

#Family4Ever:
_____
_____
_____

#H4E TEACHABLE MOMENT - RESOURCE OVERLOAD

With so many books, philosophies, web resources, colleges, and self-help outlets, it can be overwhelming trying to decide how to live. It can be even harder to articulate what we stand for, **but articulate we must!** We become our words, and our words and the actions that support them give us the greatest opportunity in this life to impact the world. Whether we feel led only to be a positive impact for our families or if we feel led to travel the world taking care of others, **our fulfillment lies in the desires of our heart. We were made to discover these desires and apply them each and every day.**

THE RISE OF THE FAMILY

The Holy Family is our greatest example of how a family should function. Joseph, as the head of the household and the **Patriarch**, was bold in the protection and provision of his family, yet he made many sacrifices for the benefit of the family and for the overall common good. He exemplified leadership and service at the same time and was also obedient to the will of God. Mary was committed to her family and was obedient to the will of God. She did not think she was worthy to carry out God's mission, but she humbly accepted the task and carried it out.

Mary could be our very best example of the strongest woman ever. She cared for her son and never left his side. Funny how women typically never abandon their children or responsibilities but weak men often run from responsibilities. Mary was a strong example for other women and was a great **Matriarch** of the family.

Joseph and Mary put God at the center of all of their plans. **There is nothing more beautiful or powerful** than a husband and a wife committed to stay together for the benefit of one another through thick and thin and who decide to raise their children together forever. Jesus gives us a great example of how to behave inside of the family as a child. Often we only think of Jesus as a full-grown man, but Jesus was quite a young man who started teaching about the ways of God as early as twelve years old. At twelve, Jesus was already making moves. That is when he tapped into the industriousness of his relationship with God. **Regardless of how old you are, the Holy Family is a tremendous example of family, and we should think of this more as it will help guide our families.**

The family is just a collection of individuals unless someone effectively leads the group in purpose and planning. When children are very small, parents are constantly focused on the basic needs of their children. Parents physically protect their children from harm and make sure they are properly fed and cleaned. As a child grows up, they will become less dependent on the day-to- day needs we provide for them and **they will be seeking a personal relationship with us. "Coaching" is a powerful word for parents.** If parents have a spirit of mentorship for their children, a child can feel empowered, loved, and appreciated. **There are many parenting styles that can be effective.** The most important thing is that a child will share what they are truly thinking with you so that you have the opportunity positively influence them. If "coaching" doesn't feel like the right word to you, then "parenting" and "mentoring" must be synonyms when raising children. Kids typically know when they make mistakes and it is our job to help them not repeat the same mistakes.

I find that a family with a defined culture will be a happier place. Now don't think that my children don't fight with each other because that would be misleading, but **my children know where the boundaries are.** We reinforce those boundaries often, especially when our children forget. It is called the **Culture of Legacy**, which is how we are responsible for creating the culture of our family. **If you don't like your family culture, change it.** If you like it, honor it and pass it on to the next generation. Regardless, you do need a plan, and the best part of a plan is when you can communicate it. Here is an example of a plan that you can use or even make it your own in the resource section:

BUILD YOUR FAMILY LEGACY PLAN

Family Mission (a family mission statement must be timeless and worthy to pass onto the next generation)

Ours: To Lead, Equip, and Inspire Others

Family Example: The Holy Family

Daily Gratitudes: **B**egin each Day **I**n **G**ratitude (Think **BIG**)

Read the Bible: 5 Minutes a Day is all it takes

Pray for: Our Family, Ourselves, and Others

The Seay Family likes to live, learn, love, and have fun adventures while spending quality time together all focused on **Faith, Family, Fitness, and Business and Community** Contributions. Unconditional love lives in our home. This is our legacy and how we **"SEAYS THE DAY"**.

Principles: To be who we are

             To have harmony

             To learn from our mistakes

             To leave things better than we found them

             To listen and seek to understand one another

             To maintain self-control and find a peaceful way

             To respect others and not interrupt

             To not say "can't" because we can

***

Writing out the plan is the easiest part, but living it...that is the hardest part. But without a written plan to begin with, you are starting at a disadvantage or you are continuing to live with broken or weak intentions. Chances are that you won't even start if you don't write it down.

      Mom and Dad have to be working hard together on this, and they also **STILL** have to be working hard on their own marriage as husband and wife to reach the objective of raising a successful family. Kids like to know that their mom and dad love each other so moms and dads **also need a vision for themselves as a couple** so have "Couple Goals" too. A lot of marital conflict goes away when each spouse can recite the goals of the other spouse.

FAMILY OBJECTIVES

Amanda and I have a loving and expressive marriage that sets a positive example for our children. We experience daily affections for one another and have weekly date nights. We have monthly date nights for our children. Our children have a personal relationship with Jesus Christ, and they love one another and respect our family unity, even when it hurts. They respect one another as siblings and respect us as parents. Even during times of conflict, they know the family is important and the family is forever.

We all know that there is no such thing as a "normal" or "perfect" family. Life is real, and families have a lot of moving parts to say the least and if people are involved, there will certainly be miscommunications. While families don't have to strive to be perfect, **they can strive to be strong**— but that won't happen by accident. **Dads have to lead families the right way, and that does not include bullying or abusing the mom.** Weak men bully their wives mentally and physically—and if physically, you may need a trip to prison, and I know some folks that are willing to drive you there. Parents have to work together to exemplify a good environment so that kids not only have a good life growing up themselves, but that they can learn a good model of family to teach their own children in the future.

All too often, Dads shy away from being great leaders at home. **They want to be champs at work but act like chumps at home.** Another plaque at work, another crack at home. Now we must be careful not to stereotype moms and dads in a certain way because the family of the past is not the family of today. Today, it is common to find both parents working, not because they need dual incomes but because both Mom and Dad have professional goals.

There is nothing wrong with goals, but it is important that the family's goals always come first. **Don't let anyone lie to you. Both marriage and raising a family** take tremendous time, effort, and intention as well as attention. I think it is flat-out heroic for a man or woman to control their schedule and appointments around their family commitments. And what is even more heroic is having the swagger to be able to communicate this to your employer, employees, or clients because when you stand on this conviction for your family, even in today's terms, you draw the line and let people know who they are dealing with. Maybe you lose a job. Maybe you lose a client, but you will not lose your family.

Parents are losing families every day, and divorce attorneys will attest that business is booming. Sometimes things go as planned, and sometimes they don't. When things don't go well and they are continuing not to go well, there is no shame in contacting a family therapist or counselor. **Some of the best families use therapy to get things back on track.** There was a time when marriage counseling and family counseling was necessary for our family. We are grateful to know that we always have the ability to go back should we need an outside perspective. **Don't let pride keep you from therapy.** The right therapist can truly help you and your family. Implement what you learn in therapy and it will work. It is that simple. People can change behaviors. Don't let things get so out of control that you can't see your way back. **Family is forever and deserves our best efforts. Who is going to cry at your funeral?**

#H4E TEACHABLE MOMENT
If You Want to "Be the Man"

Men: **If you want to "Be the Man," you have to "Be" The Man.** I don't know how else to put it, but you can't be a hero unless you are willing to do heroic things. Things like remember your wife's love language even if it sounds like Greek. Things like doing the small things that if left undone will drive her crazy. Real men fold laundry and teach their kids how to do the same. Real men plan special nights out with their wives and children. Real men spend just as much time studying family development as they do their financial investments. Being a real man is really about serving others. Why do we work so hard to be cool to our golf buddies or college roommates but say the most horrible things to the women who love us or the kids that adore us? Listen, kids won't adore you forever if you disrespect that relationship and your wife won't be too far behind.

I see a lot of broken and weak men in the making because they were poorly raised or "shadow-boxed" raised by weak men. Yes, the fruit doesn't fall far from the tree either way and the clothes won't make the man, but the fabric of their character will. It is never too late to start being a better father or husband, but you have to decide to be a warrior. Would you let someone walk into your home and harm your family? Absolutely not, so why are you slowly choking them out by your own lack of right conduct at home? Turn the choke-hold into a hug and set things right. Ask for forgiveness, call a counselor, make things happen, and save your family.

Reclaim what has been lost. Repair the breach and BE THE MAN.

#H4E TEACHABLE MOMENT
If You Want to Be Superwoman

If you want to "Be Superwoman," you have to "Be" Superwoman. In a head-to-head, box-office comparison, according to the website By the Numbers, Superman grossed $667 million globally in 2017. Wonder Woman grossed $812 million. How did Wonder Woman outperform Superman? Well, it could be that Wonder Woman got tired of waiting on Superman to show up and do something to make her life better. You can't really blame Wonder Woman. I mean, she has a good head on her shoulders and impressive skills herself, but if she can't find a hero to honor her, cherish her, and to do some important things that a man should do for a woman, well c'mon, she ain't going to wait forever. I mean, she has an invisible jet if you have forgotten.

Women are going to take matters into their own hands and rightly so. Gone are the days that women sit around and wait for the man on the white horse. The man on the white horse often gets lost, stays too long at the bar, and isn't really taking too much pride in himself or the legacy he has the power to create. Instead, women have gotten used to men leaving a wake of incompetence, disinterest, insecurity, and selfishness. Now double down with the current headlines of sexual harassment, absentee fatherhood, and all the associated misbehaviors and you can't fault any woman for not having faith in the men around them. Now, the immortal declaration in the US Declaration of Independence may state that all men are created equal, but based on conduct alone, we know that all men are not created equal. Some dads are in, some dads are out, and some dads are way out. I think one of the saddest realities for a child is when they mature to the age when they can truly evaluate the credibility of their fathers and realize that they don't really have a good dad. That must be a very hard pill to swallow for a young man or young lady. Since their births, they have loved their fathers. Their daddy is a hero. They can do no wrong. They are funny, they smell good and they are really cool. But as they grow, neglected children wise up and they start to see a pattern emerging… a pattern of disappointment. It cuts like a knife through their souls, and every time Father Schmuck doesn't come through on his word, he cuts freshly the souls of their mother (likely ex-wife by now).

Ladies, no one blames you for giving up on men. I would too. But please know this: there ARE good men out there. There are men who had good parents raise them or good role models that stepped in. There are good men who understand chivalry, respect, integrity, sacrifice, and dedication to not only a wife but to the family. The good men have muscles. They can make the world a better place, but every time they are building up their wives, their children, or their community, they have to explain to their children or to women that they respect, a new headline of how our national leaders or celebrities have disrespected a position of authority or taken advantage of a woman or even a child. These good men have to turn their eyes away from noble causes and worthy goals to cover their ears of the noise of men falling like exploding trees more fiercely in the midst of a raging forest fire. They have to stop what they're doing to take the phone calls of the broken men who made the horrible mistakes and now are crying to the good men on the phone asking for help. Alas, the good men give the help and do what they can as much as they want to strangle the caller because they told them to turn away from the destructive behavior a long time ago, when they could see the cracks in the armor first starting to appear.

These failing men are white men just as much as they are black men. These failing men are young failing men as much as they are old failing men. They have so much more in common than they will ever believe. Regretfully, they have failure in common. It was alcohol's fault. No it wasn't. It was the recreational drugs. Nope, not even close. But it was the attention the woman gave you. Nah, I don't think so. Unfortunately, it was the choice the failing man made. Yes, that is the answer. Ladies, whether you are young or old, black or white, tall or short, it doesn't matter. God made you to have more in a man. He made you to be honored and supported by wonderful men.

I am sorry if your father was a poor example. I am sorry if one of your coaches or boyfriends took advantage of you. I am sorry if someone stole your dreams, but please know this, there are good men out there. Good men that say sensitive things toward women. Men that kiss women like they love them and hold their children with undying dedication flowing from their soul. Yes, good men live on this planet, and they have two feet planted firmly on the ground. I know where they are. Fellas, I can take you there if you want to be one. You have to be willing to walk through the insecurity of the schmucky men that will try to keep you in their dark world, but on the other side, there is a righteous power and peace that will polish you off and build you up.

I love strong women. Strong women pushed through the weeds a long time ago. The last thing I can do is fault a strong woman for looking down on men. The only thing I can say to that is did you build that impression on the weak men that you know around you or in the media? Fair assessment on your part, but know good men exist and we are making some noise now with a new generation of men. A new generation of tried and true principles. Principles that honor women, protect children, and build up communities whether black or white. Ladies, keep the light burning. We are on our way and you can bet we are hustling to get there as fast as possible.

#H4E TEACHABLE MOMENT
Young Adults See You

Today the youth of America has mixed messages about who to look up to, and that's a problem. The problem will continue, but only if parents, teachers, coaches, athletes, and performers allow it to continue. The ME can easily become WE, but we can't get there until we find out WHO can make a difference. I have a pretty good idea about WHO can, and I will share it with you in the CommUnity Section of this book. If this book is in your hands and you can honestly say you are a young person with some influence, please spend some serious time reflecting on your platform and the power that you might have. What if the power to inspire the youth is right at your finger tips. What if your Twitter Account or YouTube Channel could be a place of hope and morale boosting? What if your Instagram not only made you look cool and fun, but also helped others understand that they were cool and fun too and that their young lives could do great things. Platforms are powerful. Please honor yours. I heard a celebrity once say that she didn't feel any responsibility to do great things for society just because her music made her famous. I wish that young lady didn't have any influence, but she does. I wish she had a different perspective on her platform and will hope that she comes around. Maybe with time, she will honor her platform.

There is no better time to change or even fine-tune your family culture than right now, so here is a process that can help you build a better family culture, but can also be used in your business or in any organization from The White House to your house.

#Family4Ever Mission - To Make Your Family Awesome or Even More Awesome on a Daily Basis

Model A Great Example of a Family That Inspires You:
Example:
The Holy Family

Your Example:

Positive Way to Start Your Day:
Example:
Daily Gratitude – Count your blessings, no matter how small like your heartbeat or even the ability to smile.

Your Example:

Pray for others – Pull for your brothers and sisters, parents and other people around you. God has plenty for everyone. Abundance is a mindset.

Your Example:

A Family Mission Statement must be timeless and worthy to pass onto the next generation.

The Seay Family likes to live, learn, love and have fun adventures while spending quality time together all focused on Faith, Family, Fitness, Business and Community Contribution. Unconditional Love lives in our home. This is our legacy. We lead, equip and inspire.

Principles:

To be who we are
To have harmony
To learn from our mistakes
To leave things better than we found them
To listen and seek to understand one another
To maintain self control and find a peaceful way
To respect others and not interrupt
We don't say "can't" because we can

Understand the Value behind all the talks and the lessons provided by parents. You have to choose to see the value in each lesson.

Write Your Family4Ever Mission Statement, then LIVE IT!
A Family Mission Statement must be timeless and worthy to pass onto the next generation.

_____
_____
_____
_____
_____

Your Principles (The Character of Your Family):

_____
_____
_____
_____
_____

The #Family4Ever Story
If you haven't see the #Family4Ever Video, please take a moment to watch it.
You can find the link over in Instagram @Hustle4EverLife

3. #FITNESS4EVER

I love physical fitness and I like to move daily. I like it for a few reasons. I like to feel strong and I like to work out all of the tremendous nervous energy I have each day. I tell you this because I am also humbled to think that while I hope to maintain this practice my entire life, I also recognize that I can't do the things now that I used to do in my twenties. I believe my body is a temple. I believe your body is also a temple. Good health is certainly a blessing. Sometimes poor health cannot be avoided due to family history or plain misfortune and disabilities. Those situations are beyond our control, but for the things that are within our control (diet, exercise, and positive thinking), we can use all the great information available today to live healthier **and longer lives.**

We have the power to choose how we will shop at the grocery store and how we will order at a restaurant. We have the power to binge drink and eat or not binge drink or eat. **Free will is a beautiful thing, and it impacts so many areas of our lives, but especially our bodily health.** We hear that we are overworked, stressed out, and obese in America. You have seen all the statistics I am sure, but **we are simply a product of the decisions we have made about our health and fitness.**

Have you ever been too tired to do something? Too tired to play with your kids or too tired to give your best at work or at home? You know what I mean. When you really wanted to exert more effort but you just couldn't find the strength? It is typically a cycle that needs to be broken. You can't have more energy until you train your body to produce more energy. **Often the best feeling of accomplishment we can have on a daily basis is the way we feel after a workout.** When we are leaving the gym after a workout or cooling down after a run, we know that we have done something good for ourselves. We know that the sweat we see and feel was an investment in ourselves.

If you currently don't exercise, you probably think you won't enjoy it, but you just haven't found the form of exercise you like yet. You can take routine walks with your spouse, children, or even a neighbor. You can join a gym and take specific classes. You can find a barre or yoga studio or even take martial arts. **Your body simply needs to move to help you feel better.** Don't worry about only looking better. Start with something small, but please do start. **The human body was not designed to sit around.**

My routine consists of early-morning workouts. I enjoy that time for myself. **I use it as my personal development time.** I have tried many types and styles of physical fitness from group classes and working out alone. Years ago, I settled on working out alone, and I also work out at my home. After years of going to gyms to exercise, I decided to try working out at home when my first child was born. While I used to get up early, go to the gym, shower afterward, and head to work, when my first child arrived, the quiet morning routine was long gone. I created a gym in my garage. I would take the baby monitor out to the garage and would work out as long as a non-crying child would allow. I would usually get a treadmill run in and a few weights in and then it would come to a screeching halt when my first child, Emma, would wake up. Since my wife breastfed all through the night, I just couldn't ask her to get up in the morning too. Since she needed her rest, the gym routine had to change. **Funny how when we give up something we love for someone we love, you get a better result anyway.**

Aside from being amazingly hot in the Charleston summer out in the garage, the home workouts grew on me and I started to love the practicality of rolling out of bed, not even looking in the mirror, and heading out to the garage. I started acquiring modest gym equipment over the years, and by the time we moved to our next home, I had moved the gym inside into the air conditioning. My wife joined me, and most mornings even still to this day, we work out (at the same time, but individually of course) in the early morning together. Not only is it efficient, but it doesn't allow us to make excuses about going to a gym.

I highly recommend the Bowflex by Nautilus and you can likely find one for a few hundred dollars on eBay along with free weights, etc. **You don't have to work out at home, but this system has worked for me for years and it protects the workout—meaning it greatly increases the likelihood that the workout will occur before a busy day robs you of your personal fitness time.** Just make sure that you discover a system and consistently exercise.

Your body, mind, and soul will thank you for it. Your routine is your routine, and that is all that matters.

Try to find something you somewhat enjoy as well so that you can increase your chances of sticking with it. Some people like a variety of physical activities during the week, and that's great. I like to go for an early Sunday morning bike ride each week. I look forward to it all week. **Just find what works for you.** The most important thing is to find something. Exercise is something that can truly be an amazing release for you. Our bodies are temples, and we should treat them the right way.

Physical fitness doesn't mean that you have to have every muscle ripped and bulging, but as you age, you will desire strength and stability. Simply walking with confidence will become important to us all at some point, so make sure you can defend the workouts you are choosing each day. Make sure you can explain how they are helping you build long-term strength and flexibility.

Here is how to best approach the mental side of having #Fitness4Ever:

#Fitness4Ever "MINDMAP" by Coach Seay
THE HEALTH & NUTRITION THINKING THAT CHANGES LIVES™

Why Do We Do What We Do?

If we do not control our habits, our habits will begin to control us and ultimately define us. Habits should work for us, not the other way around.

How often do you examine your fitness and health goals in relation to your daily exercise and nutritional decisions to fairly access if your habits are positive or negative? Are your habits growing you or decaying you?

TODAY IS THE DAY to claim good habits and connect your actions to your desired result.

1) Think BIG! (Begin In Gratitude)

I AM grateful for _____

(Example: I AM grateful for the ability to freely move my body and feed myself.)

2) Visualize Your Success

Claim, affirm and believe a vision of how you are going to look and feel when you have obtained eating habits, a fitness routine and the body image that you desire.

WRITE IT OUT IN A POSITIVE TONE AND SENTENCE:

(Example: I AM proud of my physical transformation and the new found strength and energy I feel to move with excitement today and serve the people around me that I love and appreciate.)

3) Literally See Your Success With The Use Of An Image

Find an image of the desired body type that you will accomplish. You can use a picture from a magazine or a past image of yourself when you were most proud of your body. Just make sure it is a positive picture with the person doing a positive activity like running, walking, laughing or walking on the beach.

CUT AND GLUE YOUR IMAGE HERE:

> GLUE YOUR IMAGE HERE. TYPE IN "Healthy Body Images" in your search engine and select "images" once the results return and look for a good picture that represents where you want to go. Then, insert that image here simply by printing it, cutting it to the size of this box and use glue or tape to put it over this text. Reference this image often even if you hang this sheet on your wall or put it in your gym bag. Look at it before, during or after your work out or hang it anywhere that can help you avoid sabotage (Ex. in the kitchen).

(Example: I have upgraded my image over the years. I have used pictures I have found from the internet and I typically just use a picture with no head or face so that I increase my chances that I envision myself accomplishing the results I want to obtain.)

4) Express WHY you desire your improved health and body

When you know why you are doing something and you recall the motivation behind your actions, you use certainty to push yourself past your fears and weak moments when self-sabotage is most likely. Define and recall your reason "WHY".

WHY are you accomplishing better health/nutritional habits for your mind and body?

(Example: I KNOW that I deserve to feel comfortable in my own skin and that I deserve to be healthy and strong so that I can reach my personal and professional dreams and say YES to all the good things life has to offer me. I was created to be great and I will not accept being mediocre anymore. I will become the best version of myself no matter what! I EXPECT an improved life now and am CERTAIN that it is happening to me. I am worthy to receive it!)

My WHY Theme is _____
(Example: A Theme is a word or tagline that gives you quick motivation. My WHY Theme is "Execution", which reminds me that a life with only intention and not specific action steps is just talk and not walk.)

#Fitness4Ever GOALS - Name your specific goals through affirmative statements:
(Example: I AM 15 pounds lighter by the end of this year and walk/run 10 minutes more each day.)

_____
_____
_____
_____
_____
_____

My Definition of #Fitness4Ever Success is:
(Example: If you look back on your fitness and health efforts one year from today, what would you have accomplished to consider yourself successful? Define your OWN success and then go get it!

It is one year from today and my #Fitness4Ever SUCCESS looks like this:
_____
_____
_____
_____
_____
_____

> You have a choice to make. Choose Health, Vigor and Energy for Life. Exhaustion, Low Self Esteem and Poor Body Image are the results if you do nothing. Run away from this pain. Once you breakthrough the mediocrity of your past, you will cherish your exercise and nutrition. You will crave this powerful part of your daily life. Each day will be filled with passion for life!
> **YOU MUST BELIEVE IN YOUR #FITNESS4EVER AND STARTOW!**

Again, you have my permission to change the words, but the intent is the same, make a habit… keep a habit. And if you need a calendar to help with habit creation, here is another Hustle Tool:

#Fitness4Ever Calendar
"REBOOT HABIT CALENDAR" by Coach Seay

Changing Habits - Psychology

Science has shown us that if you can change a habit for 23 consecutive days, you can remap a NEGATIVE behavior to a desired behavior. Repeat the 23-day mental exercise for two additional periods of 23 days and you can close the door on going back to a bad habit or behavior. Self-Sabotage is important to avoid during a process of rewiring your choices and habits and an elevated sense of awareness is your greatest tool, so know when you are most likely to fail and be extra prepared for specific things on specific days.

You have to DECIDE.

You chose your habits. Then your habits become your behavior. This guide helps you ReBoot your Path of Wellness.

You CAN do it

Simply put, we are a collection of our decisions driven by our motivations... the things that we hold to be our beliefs and values. This is your moment to start controlling your decisions.

ReWire Your Thinking

Physical fitness and exercise is thrilling and invigorating on a daily basis. Once it is a part of your daily programming, you will appreciate it, but if you don't like the thought of exercise at this moment, this is your tool to ReWire and ReBoot.

EACH	DAY	YOU	CHOSE	YOUR	OWN	DECISIONS
					1 Today you will feel excited and motivated. Affirm Yourself!	2 Today you will still be excited and focused. Affirm Yourself!
3 SABOTAGE ALERT. Reaffirm Your WHY! This time is different!	4 SABOTAGE ALERT. Reaffirm yourself with pictures and quotes.	5 SABOTAGE ALERT. Reaffirm yourself with a positive mantra like "I AM THE BOSS!"	6 STAY ALERT TODAY	7 POSITIVE HABIT CREATION GOAL #1	8 STAY ALERT TODAY	9 STAY ALERT TODAY
10 SABOTAGE ALERT. Reaffirm Your WHY! This time is different!	11 SABOTAGE ALERT. Reaffirm yourself with pictures and quotes.	12 SABOTAGE ALERT. Reaffirm yourself with a positive mantra like "I AM FIT!"	13 STAY ALERT TODAY	14 POSITIVE HABIT CREATION GOAL #2	15 STAY ALERT TODAY	16 STAY ALERT TODAY
17 SABOTAGE ALERT. Reaffirm Your WHY! This time is different!	18 SABOTAGE ALERT. Reaffirm yourself with pictures and quotes.	19 SABOTAGE ALERT. Reaffirm yourself with a positive mantra like "I AM WORTHY!"	20 STAY ALERT TODAY	21 REWIRE GOAL #1. You DID IT!	22 STAY ALERT TODAY	23 BOOM! YOU DID IT. START OVER!

#H4E TEACHABLE MOMENT
Remain Available to Help

I have given up on being frustrated watching other people never get around to starting a workout routine or start to take daily nutritional habits seriously. I used to think I wasn't a good coach or I wasn't inspiring enough, but after years of watching human behavior, I have found peace now by understanding that you can't make anyone do anything. If someone doesn't want to get into shape, they are not going to get in shape and as hard as it is to accept this especially if you love working out and eating well, **you have to meet people where they are** and truly just offer up your best every time and then simply leave it alone. When someone is ready to get in good shape or truly appreciate your guidance and advice... that will be the time to give them your best. In the meantime, just be you and do your best with who is ready to move to the next level of self-improvement.

4. #BUSINESS/COMMUNITY4EVER – The Slash

Significance matters, and it is more important than you think. **This section is one in the same for a reason, and the slash is an important transition.** We put a tremendous amount of our identity into our work. When we work, we feel productive. **Hopefully, you enjoy your work.** My hope for you is that you actually love your work and that you are challenged, continue to grow, and take your best to the office each day. Of course, it may not be an office at all. It could be a fire truck, a hospital, or even a retirement home, but whatever profession you work in, may you work well and give it your absolute best.

Work is such a big part of who we are. Some careers earn more wealth and others earn more appreciation, but **all good work is important.**

Significance is also a part of our journey at work and beyond. Whether we work for a corporation or a small business, we identify with what we do, which could be good and bad. **For those who have taken the time to discern their time and talent, they will typically end up in a job that means something important to them or operating their own business that they love to the core of their being.** They will have pride in their work, which helps build self- confidence and personal fortitude. **They will feel like they are making a difference.** For those that don't feel like they are making a difference or living out their full potential, they will simply feel like they are punching the clock. I hope that is not you. I have lived in the "punching the clock" place before and it is horrible and like a nightmare to be candid. I wouldn't wish this experience on anyone but I know it refined me and brought me to my current fulfillment and has helped create this message for you. God worked it out on his timeline and waiting was tough, but now I appreciate it more than I ever thought when I was actually walking through it.

When I was old enough to understand what my father did for a living, I just assumed that I would do that too. I think a lot of kids are like me. If their parents were respectable and successful, their parents' careers can seem attractive, especially if you spent time going to their office or where they worked. You got to see certain things behind the scenes. As a child, you think you know, but you don't. Work probably looks easy. Wait, what do you mean you don't get a summer vacation? Well not typically. Boy, that was some bad news to discover. Sometimes assumptions can really hold us back. My dad is a great man and my mother is a great woman. They really have only tried to set my sister and me up for success for as long as I can remember. I know that is not always the case and trust me… I appreciate it. I have NOT taken it for granted. My dad often talked to me about "coming into the business" and it seemed like a pretty logical thing to do. After a successful career start with sales, I went with a start up company in New York City that failed and that lead me to the decision of joining my father's business and starting our transition back to South Carolina as my wife was about to graduate from dental school. It all seemed to make so much sense until the day I actually started working in my father's office. I tried my best to fake it, but I knew it was not the place for me. My father suggested I go see a career counselor and I was certainly up for the opportunity to discover where I needed to be to be happy at work, which I feel is extremely important since we spend so much time there each week. The discovery process was a game changer. It was like the whole world moved for me. **I felt like I was looking myself in the mirror for the very first time.**

As painful as the transitions that followed turned out to be, my father had grace beyond grace to help me get on a new path that would take me away from financial advising and more on the entrepreneurial path that has been in my soul since my birth. Today, I can say that I approach each task, job and opportunity knowing how I will behave and how I will perform and the process revealed my DNA for contribution as well and this book is certainly some of the result for internal reflection completed years ago. **My children will experience this process well before college based on my experience.** To reflect on who you are early and often is a good thing and it can keep you from making choices that may not be on the right path for how you are hard wired. **Time is limited so the sooner we get to your gifts, the better.** mentioned this section is one in the same (Business/CommUnity) for a reason however, it could easily be a whole chapter dedicated to your business life or your career. It could be about how to build a resume, how to interview, how to look for opportunities within an organization, how to apply for internal promotions, and climb to the top of an organization. It could just as easily be a chapter dedicated to actively volunteering for a non-profit board position or how to coach recreational sports for the development of children around you. All that has a place and a purpose, but **without some dedicated study of your significance and how that relates to you on a daily basis, you may be setting yourself up to miss the purpose of your creation.** Work is good, but it comes in all shapes and sizes and has different meanings to different people. What does your job or business mean to you? Do you wake up with passion for your work? Are you excited about what you are doing?

With proper planning, the hope is that we will all be in a position to retire from our primary professions one day. If you have never spent a few minutes to think about this day in the future, it can seem too abstract, but **it is a worthy and responsible goal to plan for this day at least in the financial-needs perspective.** I am not going to help you with the financial planning aspect of this (remember I didn't want to be a financial advisor☺). There are many great resources available today to help you, however when you arrive at retirement, have you thought about what you will do each day? Will you visit the Grand Canyon or move closer to loved ones? Will you spend more time volunteering or pursue a hobby that you have always wanted to try? <u>**Life is a journey of significance. We want to contribute and feel like our lives have mattered and added value to the planet, especially to our loved ones and friends.**</u>

It's easy to get too focused on our work, but that work as we know it usually will end—and then what? Will you have a crisis of significance and wander aimlessly into retirement, seeking purpose? You don't want that. You don't want to find yourself in a position where you are questioning what your level of contribution has been to this life experience. Yes, life is busy, but you don't want to get so busy that you don't take some time to discern your unique talents and motivations to ensure they align with all the areas of your life so you can live a balanced and well-rounded life. **Success isn't a fully funded retirement.** That may be a piece of it, but that is not how you establish and leverage your significance for your own fulfillment and the fulfillment of others around you. **You can volunteer now. You can contribute now. You can be significant now and experience a fulfilled life's purpose with a little time and attention spent examining your contribution on a daily basis.**

Something in the discovery process will most likely involve volunteer work in your community on some level, and if it does not, **it should.** Caring for others is a great way to get outside of yourself. There are so many ways to look out for those that need help. It could be disadvantaged youths or adults. It could be as easy as donating money to as complex as identifying a less-fortunate person you know and providing resources for them to make it through a rough patch.

From soup kitchens to the Goodwill Organization, the opportunities to give back to others are endless. **Some will be easy and some will be hard, but you don't have to wait until you retire to get involved with worthy causes. The strangest thing is that you will experience a new appreciation of gratitude when you volunteer and serve the needs of others.**

WHEN YOU STRIKE CONTRIBUTION GOLD

In 2015, a very good friend of mine (TJ Van Thullenar) and I started Souldier Week for Boys, which is a camp for boys ages eight to seventeen years old **that promotes how to live a well-rounded life grounded in Faith, Family, Fitness, and Academics and Community.** The camp is like a mini-TED® Talks Conference for little guys to encourage authentic leadership and life success principles. At about age fourteen, we start selecting junior leaders (Souldier Elites) to help us facilitate the camp as peer leaders. The week-long camp incorporates motivational and informative presentations on various topics ranging from how to eat healthy to hand-to-hand combat. Our local S.W.A.T. team and fire department along with many others come each year to make presentations. The camp has gained popularity, and it has grown from fourteen boys to as many as seventy-eight boys as we enter the fifth year.

The camp is all volunteer led, operated by four local businessmen (and growing) who take a week off from work to positively impact these young men and promote how to do the right thing in every situation—so much so, that it becomes cool to be smart, have "righteous swagger" and care for others. **We promote the cool factor in doing the right thing.** I know I speak for all of our adult and junior leaders when I say that you really can't put into words how we feel that week, especially on the last day of camp when we pack the school gym where the camp is held and moms and dads come to hear more about what we did during the week. In the early years, I had plenty of people mention how much money we could make setting these camps up across the country. I know that is true. I see what camps cost, and I know that there is a way to turn this camp into a financial machine, but that is not our goal. Our goal is much bigger. Our goal is to build a new generation of men…**real men** taking boys and **inspiring them** on the path of righteousness as they turn into young adults. **No celebrities, just real-life heroes with real-world information that can minimize mistakes and accelerate <u>real success</u>. You have to trust me on this… <u>our way wins</u>. This approach to life cannot fail you, it sets you up for authentic success… a success that you can be proud of and know that your life has the ability to do great things not only for your own personal satisfaction, but for the benefit of others as well. We hear of win-win situations all the time, but rest assured this is the purest form of winning.**

Your contribution can come in many shapes and sizes. If you are a boxer, you could start a boxing academy for girls or you could start a sailing program for special needs children if you have experience sailing. **All you need to do is evaluate your talents and examine your heart of service to see how you can bless those around you with what you know. You don't have to wait until retirement to do this.** You can and MUST start today at least mapping out the program that you dream of starting. My friend Holly Van Thullenar wrote her Girl Power Program in the middle of the night from start to finish, so we know that when inspiration comes, it comes quickly and often completely.

You are worthy to contribute. Your past mistakes make your instruction even more valuable. **Doing good is super cool.** That is so important for children that I must repeat it and bold it again and this time underline it as well: **Doing good is super cool.** You will feel phenomenal. Even if you simply Adopt-a-Highway section in your community and clean it up regularly, you are making something better. I always tell myself, my wife, my children, and my Souldiers, **"Leave it better than you found it."** Why not? Why can't we constantly improve ourselves and improve the communities where we live along the way?

I will be the first one to tell you I consider myself ambitious, but **being overly self-ambitious is a broken model for the steward's life.** A steward takes care of not only resources they have been given, but the people that they encounter in their spheres of influence. And with the way we communicate today, you never know how your example could start a movement around the world. **You can only lead by example.** It is that simple, and all the leadership books in the world won't change that. **You can't preach integrity, authenticity, or any other buzzword without living with integrity and authenticity.** Even the weak moments in my life when I have tried to spin a business angle and try some slick new way to do something, **it hasn't worked without an authentic heart.**

What can you do to improve everyone's life around you? You must take time to inventory what time, talents, and treasures are already in your hands, **imparted directly from God.** If you simply take the time to inventory these things, you will discover something good that you can share with your community or even the world.

Don't wait any longer. Hustle for your community or someone in need around you. You will never know how good it feels to have helped other people until you can look back on the helping you just did. It is probably the highest feelings of reward in this life. Even if you act like it wasn't a big deal, **your heart, your mind, and your soul will be telling you differently.** You will have touched a funny three-letter word called **JOY, one of the most misunderstood words in the English language.**

#H4E TEACHABLE MOMENT – VOLUNTEER LIKE A BALLER

How much time do you have to volunteer? If the gut reaction answer is "none," then what can you do to create more time to volunteer? Can you squeeze out one day per week or even just an hour a month? **Start somewhere, but just start.** Once you assess your time, ask yourself, "What volunteer opportunities exist around me?" **Do you have a unique talent or skill that can be a blessing to others?** Why do guys sponsor disadvantaged young men thorough organizations like the YMCA? Because those men likely are good at coaching sports or being positive role models. Women can do the same. If you are stumped, ask yourself, "Do I know anyone that volunteers?" If so, ask that person out for a coffee to learn more about why they do it. Ask them how they got into volunteering and, most importantly, what **INSPIRED** them to volunteer.

THE SIGNIFICANCE MELTDOWN

This is the slash. It is a two-edged slash. This is why Business/CommUnity are in the same section so pay attention here. Significance is the quality of being worthy of attention or worthy of importance. Work, work, work, retire, hate life, look back and have regrets, pick out a casket, and BOOM—Game Over. Barf. This is not the destination you want to set yourself up for. How valuable is life experience? Too valuable to quantify. In all my years of leadership, there have been times when I led and times when I followed. I am grateful that I can enjoy both roles.

Contributing to a larger goal will sometimes give you a driver role and sometimes it will give you a ride in the passenger seat. Regardless of style, circumstance, or even the very goal itself, the significance of what is trying to be accomplished is very important to whether something will succeed or fail and create a fulfilling experience for those who decide to contribute toward a mutual goal. There is tremendous importance in understanding significance. **The most important significance to understand is our own significance.**

I cannot stress to you enough the importance of **the slash**. This is the slash between Business or Work and Community aka **Business/CommUnity** in the #Hustle4Ever Way of Life. **This slash is way more important than even the hashtag! The slash can't wait.** The slash must NOT wait. "When I retire, I will have more time to volunteer." Have a bologna sandwich already. **Waiting is exactly the opposite thing you want to do.** I have seen it time and time again. **A person waits until retirement to contribute to the community and then when it is time to pick a cause, nothing inspires them so they feel like they don't have anything to contribute anymore and they can sink into depression or even worse, into the land of "no purpose". RUN!** Lack of purpose is a motivation killer, and it is the way we think about our significance (or lack thereof) that keeps us strong, young, and jumping out of bed in the morning.

What would it be like to find yourself only inspired enough to turn on the television in your later years and sit on the couch? Do you think you might get depressed? Do you think you are making anything happen anymore or are you just spectating from the sidelines at that point? No. **You do not want this.**

Mind, body, and soul…they are all connected. **The aging process is real.** It is going to happen, and may we all live long lives full of adventure and joy.

The slash is your key to leverage your entire life. The slash should be used today and every day to maintain your significance and to better the world. If you don't know where to start, then just think like I do: **"leave it better than you found it."** You need not look any further than your neighbor's yard to see that you can contribute immediately at any point in time. Is there an elderly woman or man on your street that could use some help with something? Have you noticed something loose somewhere? Help and tighten.

The moral of the story is get to work on the slash. Sure, if you want to really sit down and reflect on a major way to contribute, then make it a real goal-planning process, but in the meantime, pick up trash, sponsor a child, or throw a high five, but get to hustling on your slash. And while you are considering the slash, reflect on "The Dash" too:

THE DASH by Linda Ellis:

I read of a man who stood to speak at the funeral of a friend. He referred to the dates on her casket from beginning to the end. He noted that first came the date of her birth and spoke of the following date with tears, but he said what mattered most of all was the dash between those years. For that dash represents all the time that she spent alive on earth and now only those who loved her know what that little line is worth.

For it matters not, how much we own, the cars, the house, the cash, What matters is how we live and love and how we spend our dash.

So think about this long and hard; Are there things you would like to change? For you never know how much time is left that can still be rearranged.

If we could just slow down enough to consider what is true and real and always try to understand the way other people feel.

And be less quick to anger and show appreciation more and love the people in our lives like we have never loved before. If we treat each other with respect and more often wear a smile, Remembering that this special dash might only last a little while.

So when your eulogy is being read with your life's actions to rehash...

Would you be proud of the things they say about how you spent your dash?

Man, I love that poem. Gets me every time. In closing out the CommUnity Section, I want to share a concept with you that I feel has the power to end racism and hatred in our world today, thus creating real CommUnities. We can make fun of Miss America Competitions all day when "World Peace" is now the cliché joke (heck, I laugh too), but I do believe Dr. Martin Luther King's Dream was God inspired and we must continue to dream the dream. There is still work to be done, unfortunately.

Here is an opportunity to take some notes in this section:

#Business/CommUnity4Ever:

#H4E TEACHABLE MOMENT - THE ACCEPTANCE ENVELOPE

People are going to make mistakes. Your spouse is going to make a mistake. Your children are going to make mistakes. Your teacher at school might actually make a mistake. Your dog or cat might even make a mistake. Mistakes, miscommunications, poor word choices, and eye rolls don't mean that the plank needs to come out and the sharks alerted fresh meat is on deck. What if we just decided to accept people upfront rather than make other people work so hard to be accepted?

I don't mean to suggest that respect does not have to be earned, but what I am talking about here is attempting to disable the "snap-judgy trigger" in your brain that you use on a daily basis. Snap judgments can be too absolute. I like unconditional love…until you have reason to make it conditional. Giving someone the benefit of the doubt can certainly clap back on you, but usually a moderately reasonable person will appreciate building a relationship based on authenticity, trust, respect, and some occasional laughter. Good times.

Don't you like the way certain people just make you feel good? We all know people who just make us happy or make us laugh and smile, even if on the inside. I aim to be one of those people. **I wish I could say that I was always that person. I am not.** I CAN always chose to be that person, but I know that some days, I am going to be lazy with my words and even worse… lazy with my thoughts. Well, the good news is that I can literally start again as soon as I put a period here. Ta-da. OK, reboot. Seriously, I can give my best right now again and never let it go from this moment forward. Yes, it may be a challenge, but I am going to reach for the stars! If I kept score of each time a friend or acquaintance disappointed me, I would be running out of paper to keep score with, but I would also be running out of humans to spend time with.

Funny how few of us are thinking we make mistakes in this very moment.

Dude… so arrogant (you are). **But think about it like this, if you decided a friendship was over at the first sign of a disagreement over a restaurant choice or road trip destination, you wouldn't get very far on the relationship journey. How about if you decided now that at the first sign of a mistake or really stupid comment made by a friend, you were going to laugh and not go to war in the moment and then clarify how you felt about the comment later when you could get that person alone, how much less conflict would there be in this life?** I would venture to guess much less, but don't judge me yet!

One-on-one communication can be the key to all relationship success when we decide to take care in how we use our words. When multiple people and larger groups start to get together, without proper facilitation or a happy-go- lucky peacemaker on the job, you can see little discords turn quickly into nooses if you aren't careful. Words move quickly around this planet, and the bible tells us that the tongue can be a tool or a weapon and we aren't talking about any piercings in that slippery thing, **we are talking about how you choose to use it.** Make a conscious effort to evaluate how you are thinking and then you will quickly become aware of how you are speaking.

Do everything within your power to speak with life (speaking positive things into existence) and be a source for good vibes in life. If you find you need to express yourself in a more forceful way, then you probably want to call for a small conversation on the side and not create a spectacle (most likely of yourself). **The Acceptance Envelope Concept is super cool.** You are going to accept the humanity of the other person you are communicating with rather than quickly judging a comment as one swift act of condemnation forever to crush the little head of the offender. Cool heads prevail, and someone (yes, you) needs to make, keep, and spread the peace. One kiss-of-death move that can ignite a situation? Send a text message about the issue when what it really deserves is a conversation. Please think twice before you pull the text trigger.

I can think of many times when people knew I needed to address a particularly hard situation and they asked when and how I was going to address it. My answer has always been, "When the time is right to have a proper discussion." Sometimes the time is just not right to have a serious discussion.

Humbly, sometimes, you need to further examine and reflect on the details or your own behavior to make sure you haven't made up a story in your own mind about the reality of the situation. I won't belittle the text or email heavy generation of today because it is beyond convenient for us all, however, person to person contact is never going to go out of style if you consider yourself a real relationship hustler. Technology has changed many of the ways that we communicate, but proper communication and responsible communication will always prevail. Extroverts may prefer face-to- face while introverts may prefer detailed, thoughtful emails or handwritten notes. **The important thing to remember is that words matter, so use them wisely.**

BELIEF BLOCK

We've all heard of writer's block. Even if you are not a writer, you know what that means. Have you ever heard of "belief block"? Probably not because I just made it up, but you will understand what I mean as soon as I tell you. Our minds are muscles, are they not? Yes, they are, and we aren't always fully in control of them. If we were, how great could we become? How significant could this one life experience become? Could you align the desires of your heart with the reality that exists around you?

Belief block is real and you have experienced it at some point in your life or may be experiencing it now. It is when you don't truly think you can do or experience something. You don't think you can have true love or be successful, for example. The main problem with this belief is that you don't truly understand the definition of love or success or anything for that matter because you have never taken the time to create the vision of your life based on a real definition of success. Without this vision, you are not going to be able to ring that bell at the end of your life and look back and feel as if you really "made it." I can't let that happen to you because I won't let it happen to me.

PLACE A PREMIUM ON ACTION

I would love (oh yes, we will talk about love later because it is greatly misunderstood and the word often is abused) to support all that I am writing here with relevant scientific, mathematical data and statistics because I certainly have a thing for spreadsheets, but I have already read those types of books for you. I know what happens when 93 percent of this happens to 48 percent of that. And you would not believe what happens 23 percent of the time when people achieve 10 percent of nothing referenced here because there is a simple math equation that we are going to build on and carry the one on—and here it is: **when you only talk and don't walk, you don't really go on the journey of your life and discover what you are doing here.**

This can apply to anyone of any race or creed or background or upbringing. If you never get off "start," you simply don't go anywhere. Now "start" for you may really suck because it may include some daunting challenges ahead, but unless you have already diligently pursued, pondered, and recognized your full potential, then there is work to do and work is not free, easy, or cheap. Time is money, and money is time. Both are limited and won't last forever. While you are holding this book or thinking of what you have read after you put it down, please consider it an investment in yourself. **YOU ARE WORTH THE INVESTMENT OF PERSONAL DEVELOPMENT.**

THE COMPARISON MODEL IS BROKEN

Rubbernecking is for the birds (if birds have necks☺?). How many times have you said that you were not going to look at the traffic accident that had you backed up in traffic, but as soon as it is finally your turn to pass the wreck you took a peek? We are in love with this broken concept of comparison and success principles that flow from the glossy magazine covers whispering, "Psst, hey, look here! This is what success looks like." Well, I am going to help you refute that lie. **There isn't enough time left in your life to waste one single minute, especially chasing the fool's gold that attaining someone else's success is going to feel just as good for you (should you actually attain it).** C'mon, we are so much smarter than that, yet we fall for it again and again and again.

No one can keep up with the Jones because the Jones family never even existed in the first place and that is a fact. Even if they did, they wouldn't have been happy because they were just trying to keep it all together to give the illusion that they had it all together. It was an illusion all along simply based on a comic strip of how to out do your neighbors. Keeping the grass green on your side of the fence is truly hard work, so roll up your sleeves because your grass is about to green up.

EXPERIENCE IS THE BEST TEACHER

Coach Lee wanted me to play varsity my freshman year. You should have seen this team. They were huge and full of talent. Junior varsity practice started a few weeks after varsity, so in the meantime I practiced with the varsity team. It was a great experience, but I was a step slow and not as strong as I wanted to be. I never discussed it with Coach Lee, but once junior varsity practice started, I simply started attending JV practice and stopped attending varsity practice. The topic never came up nor did I bring it up. I just knew that a strong year of junior varsity play was going to be better for me in the long run than hardly playing at all at the varsity level. I was a captain on the junior varsity team, and my confidence and game improved. I learned invaluable leadership skills in game- time situations and finished the season actually ready for the challenge of varsity and looking forward to the summer of training ahead.

Sometimes, experience can be the only teacher. As much as it would have been good experience to practice at the varsity level every day as a freshman, game time would have been extremely limited and I have yet to meet anyone who likes to sit on the bench. Life is about getting in the game and making plays and also making turnovers. If you can learn from your successes and your failures, you are wise beyond your years, but you have to be in the game enough to taste success and failure.

I have a special place in my heart for benchwarmers. I used to hate the thought of my teammates sitting on the bench all game long. Many times some of my teammates would only touch the ball twice per game and that was warm- up layups each half. Now, I don't fault the coach for not playing some of the bench players because if we are being honest, most of those bench players had enough talent to get on the team but they weren't the ones who had such command of our offense or defense that they could be effective when they got into the game. They also weren't the ones I would see in the off-season weight room. So on some level, while I hated to see them disappointed that they did not play at all, if we are being fair, the tenacious work ethic and desire was not there for some of these players. Tenacity can be a huge difference maker in sports and in life. **Hustle makes a difference. Hustle typically lives where no one can see it, like in the off-season.**

ENDLESS SUMMER(S)

Over the summer between my freshman and sophomore years, my training tightened up to a series of daily drills that had **most people thinking I was crazy—and I was absolutely fine with that.** Footwork drills, ball-handling drills (my mom would time me, God bless her patience), shooting drills, weight-room circuits, and increased-calorie diets. All these things were hard enough alone to do, yet put them all together and the summer of 1991 was **a great investment in myself** as well as my basketball dreams. And it paid off.

When my sophomore year began, I couldn't wait for try-outs to begin. I used the time before the tryouts to polish all my training. In the pick-up games alone, I could tell that I had made a substantial improvement to my game over the off-season. While the players were just as big and fast, I found that I was now competitive and had the self-confidence, thanks to my preparation, to impact a game.

My attitude had shifted from "I hope I can make the team" to "I am more than worthy to be here," and it showed in my game. Loose balls...mine. Defense...my favorite. Free throws...money. Jump-shot...swish. Hustle...just came standard and guaranteed.

After Coach Lee cut four hundred boys down to twenty-five initially, we were off to work. The initial weeks of practice each season were the most brutal. Coach Lee needed the roster trimmed down even more. I think he secretly was helping a few players decide to quit so that he would have less people to cut as we ultimately finished up with fifteen players. The boys that had not played on the team before and were still on the roster knew they were on the bubble and that the deck was stacked against them if they did not have a breakthrough real quick. The level of intensity was insanely high. Coach Lee was not afraid to cut returning players either, and the returners who slacked off in the off-season paid the price most times. I was always amazed to see how fat some of the guys let themselves get in a matter of five months. If they couldn't use the weight to their advantage and prove it, the weight quickly became a liability. If you showed up without stamina, let's just say it became a stigma.

Coach German was assistant coach, along with Coach Poole (who had biceps the size of a small town and literally had to cut the inside of his sleeves just to get his school shirt to fit) and Coach Smalls. All were encouraging coaches. They were tough, but they definitely cared about what they were doing and it was obvious. I remember multiple occasions when I was motivated by something that each of them said. I always felt the desire to play bigger than I was for each of them. As a player in sports, if you have ever had a coach you respected, you always want to please them on the field of competition. You want to execute what you practiced time and time again. There has always been a place inside of me that wanted the coaches' approval, but not in a political, brown-noser kind of way...in a "yes, you did what I wanted" kind of way. **I have many great memories of accomplishment that never hit the scorecard**—times in the locker room after practice when Coach Lee would recognize my effort in front of other players and use it as an example to help sharpen the overall team. **It takes a while to realize that you can actually lead others just by example. We hear that all the time, but it truly is the easiest way to lead.** I remember the day that I became comfortable accepting the praise. It made me play harder. It made me want to keep being the good example. Never did I brag. I only shared it a few times with my family, but the rest of the time, I kept my mouth shut and my head down and I think that is what made all the difference.

People want leaders and examples to follow, not braggers. People don't typically pull for braggers, but they will root, all day long, for someone they believe in and someone that inspires them—especially when they ask for advice in private and they get it. **Then, they have found a hero. Oh, how we need more heroes and the underdog hero is the natural choice for many. Be an underdog hero.**

Sometimes we have to show leadership when we least expect it. My sophomore year, I was playing at an elevated level. I was coming back to the basketball season after a solid off-season of training and was stepping up to the varsity team. My summer camps were tremendous. I outplayed juniors and seniors everywhere I went and if I couldn't out jump or out shoot them, I would simply out hustle them.

When the actual season began, the talent on our team was phenomenal. The position I played was held by a senior, but more often than not, I was using my secret weapon of hustle to outplay him on a daily basis at practice. I was not saving anything for the games because I wanted to earn more playing time, and it happened.

While in warm-ups in front of 2,000 people on the biggest game of the season, Coach German told me I was going to be starting. At first I wanted to vomit as I looked at the other team and my mind started reeling about my position assignments and defensive responsibilities, but then excitement took over. Local television sports crews were setting up, and we were about ready to play...**I don't remember anything after that, literally.**

While I wish I could tell you that I can't remember the night because of adrenaline, I can't remember it because on one of the very next warm-up drills, my teammate came the wrong way in the three-man weave and his cheekbone went square into my nose, breaking it and knocking me out cold in a pool of blood on the court. The start I had been working so hard for had been ripped away from me, and my nose was almost three inches closer to my left ear. As I started to come back to consciousness, I was disoriented and disappointed all at the same time.

I remember seeing my father standing in front of me, and he said the most life-changing thing I have ever heard. **He said, "A hero is not the person that always wins but the person who gets back up when they get knocked down."** That night was a tough pill to swallow, but to hear those impactful words...it was like when a blacksmith drops a fire-hot sword into water when the sword is ready to be completed. I have shared those words of my father many times with others when they have suffered major setbacks. I have shared those words with my own children, children of close friends, and players I have coached. **They are words absolutely to remember. Words that matter. All words matter, especially in the context of the most challenging moments of our lives.**

COMPLETING FAILURE(S)

After the nose surgery, I got to wear a really stylish nose cast that complemented my two black eyes for quite some time. One of our biggest Christmas basketball tournaments was coming up. As much as I didn't want to go, I decided to go with the team and sit on the bench. I can't remember who else on my team that was also hurt at that time, but I remember he didn't go (and the respect I lost for him because of his decision) and he stayed home for the holidays with his family. I am glad I did not make that choice because not only did I earn more respect from my teammates and coaches, I got to watch the senior that I'd replaced before the nose debacle take back his starting position. Watching that **helped me understand that grass will grow under your feet.** If my work ethic needed any solidifying, it happened as a spectator at that tournament because I was counting the days to get back on the court. We can convince ourselves that the world revolves around us at times, but that is just a lack of self-awareness. **The world keeps turning whether we are on our game or not, so we might as well be on our game to make things a better life experience.**

During my high school basketball year, there were a lot of big games and tournaments. There were long practices and weight-training sessions and some nice awards along the way, but at the end of my senior season it happened...my last game arrived. **If you haven't seen *The #Hustle4Ever Story* Video, now would be a good time to pause and watch it.** It walks you through that final high school basketball moment. I would venture to say that we all know that "ending" feeling. The moment when something is officially over or when a season of life is changing. **Boy, does life have seasons.**

In this instance, it was my last high school basketball game. I knew the season would come to an end at some point, but it didn't really hit me until we were about to be eliminated from the state playoffs and Coach Lee sent in a teammate to check me out of the game. I realized that Coach Lee was trying to recognize me, but the wave of emotions I felt as I actually stepped off the court for the last time of my high school career was almost too much to bear.

As I hugged each coach and player, I ultimately ran out of people to hug and found myself at the end of the bench with only a towel in my hand. I could feel the tears mounting. I sat down and put the towel over my head and sobbed harder than I can ever remember. **I couldn't believe that it was over.** All the years of training on campus; the hours in the weight room; the driveway; the garage; the town gyms and basketball courts around the community. **It was the first time in my life that the end of something was so significant.**

Growing up, when summer arrives, kids dart out the door and hit the sunshine. Graduating from lower schools is more about excitement than uncertainty, but the end of a high school basketball career for a guy who gave it his all yet didn't know what the next step of hoops might look like when hoops seemed to be everything…let's just say that moment was overwhelming.

During the course of the next few months, my game tape got me a few meetings to talk about playing college basketball, and I had walk-on offers from both The Citadel and the College of Charleston. I thought for sure I would be playing for one of those schools, but something was changing inside of me. I was interested in attending the University of South Carolina as I had visited the school multiple times while my older sister was there. I thought that maybe I needed a break from basketball or maybe, on the other hand, it was worth the risk to try out for the Gamecocks and see how things went.

When I got to campus my freshman year, I immediately was submerged in all the social aspects of college life and had more fun than I'd ever anticipated. I played basketball a lot in my free time, but when tryouts came and went, I was cut from the team. Only one player earned a walk-on role, a guy I knew from previous summer camps. If anyone deserved it, he did.

He lived in my dorm, and I saw how many practices and functions he had to attend. **I didn't see him smile much.** Not sure if that was just his personality or not, but I don't think he played a single minute in a game that season. I didn't regret my decision not to play college basketball. I was beginning to understand that there were plenty of leadership opportunities on campus for me—and more than enough social functions.

Over the course of the next three years, I had a blast in college. I made hundreds of new friends, joined a fraternity, played intramural sports, worked multiple jobs, held fraternity and campus leadership positions, and visited many other campuses to visit and socialize. At the same time, my grades got better each year and I became a much more focused student than I had ever been in high school. The freedom to make my own schedule with classes and work actually helped me thrive. **I am a big believer in charting your own course.**

I did date the first three years of college. As much as I enjoyed the company of all of the fun girls I spent time with, **I never felt completely satisfied.** I feel confident most of that dissatisfaction came from within and not even being close to understanding what I was looking for in a woman. So much so, in fact, that I just stopped looking and decided to have fun and enjoy the rest of college. I had one year to go. I figured I would probably move away from my college town of Columbia, South Carolina, anyway to pursue the biggest and best job offer that I knew I was bound to receive, so I didn't feel the need to start something serious with anyone.

The last summer I was in college, I decided to attend summer school to lighten my load for my final year in regard to classes. I had a few tough economics classes left, so I decided to take two classes. That allowed me to keep working as well. Columbia became a very small place in the summer. Most students left to go home for the summer or at least to get closer to the beaches, so aside from summer school students like me the Columbia bars and campus spots were pretty much a ghost town. The students that did stay would see each other all the time. That is the summer that I met Amanda for the second time.

I knew who she was. She used to date a guy I really liked before he transferred. He and I tried out for the basketball team together. He was an extremely good guard with one of the most pure shots I have ever seen in person. We both got cut, but I enjoyed getting to know him. He was a solid guy. He introduced me to Amanda around the time we tried out for the team, but I didn't see her again for years and I thought absolutely nothing of the introduction. **Funny how timing and circumstance knows so much more that we can ever hope to. God's timing has surprised me more than once in my life,** and I have learned to embrace it—in fact, the embracing of God's timing smooths out the journey.

Evidently, Amanda and her boyfriend broke up soon after I met her for the first time. I went about my way for the next few years in my fraternity social life. I was having a great time with my friends, more or less working hard and playing hard in regard to school and social events. The thought of girlfriends would cross my mind often, but as much as that idea sounded appealing, nothing seemed to satisfy me. I dated a few girls, but nothing I would call serious and I cringe inside when I think about just how immature I was during my high school and college years in regard to relationships. I can't say for sure if I recognized just how immature I was at the time, but something kept me from entering into any serious relationships, which was probably a good thing for everyone. But I did know for sure that I was dissatisfied and did have the desire to have a companion. I did know that much, but the rest was so confusing that I decided to turn this over to God and stop worrying about it. I simply started praying for my future wife and asked God to prepare the timing and to give me wisdom and patience. **He did.**

MY LOVE STORY

At first we just hung out as friends in groups. **Amanda was just a fun person to be around. This should be a major "hint" for anyone interested in a tip on how to select a life partner, by the way.** She would come over and cook dinner with me and my roommates or we would meet out in groups. We even tried to set each other up with our friends. It was almost like we had horse blinders on. **Life gives epiphanies. It's funny how horse blinders can be on until that moment that they quite suddenly fall off.**

I remember recognizing things around her apartment that needed to be fixed. Some were big things, and some were small things. Whatever they were, I felt like they needed attention not only because it was right for any landlord to address these items (my inner landlord was speaking) but because Amanda deserved to have things "set right" in her life. I am not going to go into all the family things she experienced when she was growing up because I was not there, of course, but I can tell you that I could see the effects of the fallout to understand that the stories she told me were true and certainly impacted her.

At first I felt angry about bad things that had happened to Amanda. I wanted to right so many wrongs for her. Then the more I learned, the more scared I became because I realized I might get stuck helping her pick up the pieces. I couldn't turn away though. **It was like a big layer of my own self-absorption was being pulled away for the betterment of me as a man in general.** The day we decided to start dating, it was like a new path was immediately revealed to me. **The path of satisfaction in a relationship opened up to me like something I had never seen or felt before. It probably did not appear perfect to someone on the outside, but it was perfect for me.**

Many times in my life, I have experienced droughts. **Droughts are times in our lives when one or multiple areas of our lives are just not clicking.** They can be relational, physical, financial, or the least obvious to humanity… spiritual. As much as I have experienced these droughts and have seen others in these droughts of life as well, I have also personally experienced and witnessed others experience the quenching of thirst and struggle in these droughts. From blind dates to matrimony, from pain to healing, from broke to secure, and from lost to found. Earlier I mentioned seasons. **Life has many, but a hustler will never quit. Each day brings a new hope that you are one step closer to being satisfied.** The complete man or woman will strive to honor this journey and pursue balance in each of these areas. **It is pure joy to focus on the spiritual mind first.**

As college drew to a close, real decisions came closer and closer. I was interviewing on campus for business-related jobs while Amanda was applying to dental schools. **When you know a season of life is coming to an end, the uncertainty of tomorrow can be intimidating.** What would happen to our relationship? Where would the opportunities we were pursuing take each of us? At twenty-two years of age, these were certainly some of the most grown-up decisions we had ever faced. Transitions in life are real and they can be scary.

Amanda was considering attending New York University's College of Dentistry in Manhattan. We visited together during her NYU interviews. I would be lying to you if I told you that this Southern boy wasn't overwhelmed by the city.

I had never seen anything like it. I remember telling Amanda at lunch that I didn't think that I would enjoy living in New York. She made it clear that she was seriously considering NYU and that she was committed to going to dental school. The girl has grit. She plays up in a big way. The lunch was awkward and was a downer on a trip that was set up to be a positive experience for Amanda. Looking back now, I can see how immature I really was. I must have been too comfortable and planning a pity party at the time. I had been interviewing for a position with a securities broker dealer that my father worked for in Nashville. I was expecting some sort of an offer, but that didn't come through so I found myself nearing the end of the school year without a job in hand and dealing with more uncertainty than ever before. I was shocked that I hadn't gotten the offer in Nashville. Looking back, there really was no reason on paper why I shouldn't have at least been put in their training program, but I see the reason now. At that moment in my life, I think if the comfort choice door would have opened, I may have taken it and sabotaged myself in the end. Thank God for the times I have been passed over or even cut. They weren't failures, **they were just hard pivots.**

I understand it now, but if you can't hit a curveball yet, it is probably a good idea to figure out how to. One of our last days in Columbia, I went to visit Amanda. That day changed the path of our lives forever. As I pulled up to her house, I saw her sitting on the front porch with her head down being consoled by her roommate. **I knew it wasn't good when I saw her smoking a cigarette.** She had given up smoking six months prior, and I was sure that the letter she was holding in one hand and the cigarette she was holding in the other were not an indication of good news. I parked around back and walked up to the front porch where Amanda handed me a rejection letter from her top dental school pick that would have kept us together in South Carolina. She had already been accepted to New York University's College of Dental Medicine's Program. Now she was sobbing. It was almost like she already knew my limits and was thinking that she would be heading off to dental school in New York while I would be staying behind in South Carolina. **She is just the kind of girl, teen, and now woman who gets invited and accepted to stuff, so she had not been prepared for the rejection letter.** The fact that her South Carolina dental option was no longer on the table was a shocking curveball… the kind that disappears right at the end when the batter has swung so hard for the fence that he almost comes out of his shoes swinging and has nothing to show for it. We ended up in Amanda's bedroom talking. **I was trying to console her, but I was hoping to console myself too.** What did all this mean for us? Being with Amanda was the first time I had felt complete in a relationship. It was the first time, at the age of twenty-two, that I understood true love. I remember what I was wearing in that moment. **I remember everything about that moment, and I will never forget what I said next. I don't think either of us will. I said, "I will move to New York."**

Amanda didn't know if I was joking or being serious. The scary part was that I might have been thinking the same thing, **but when it was spoken, it became real.** Over the course of the next few months, we graduated and moved our things out of Columbia. Amanda had a long-planned European backpack tour with her best friend and I had a back surgery on the immediate horizon. I moved home with my parents for the back procedure while Amanda left for her trip.

I didn't envy her trip then, but how I envy her trip now. Back in South Carolina, I started searching for job opportunities and apartments in New York. I thought I understood competition up to that point in my life, but I really had just been scratching the surface of competition.

I had a few friends in the city. I started reading tourist books about New York and watching David Letterman like he was going to give me all the answers about NYC. I started to pick up on all his New Yorker inside jokes. Three months of physical therapy and being apart from Amanda didn't go by quickly, but the day of our move—or at least starting our move—to New York City finally arrived. I flew to Washington, DC, to meet Amanda and spend a few weeks at her best friend's house before we drove together into Manhattan. I look back and laugh because Amanda was so fiercely independent that she would not let me drive the rental box truck. I begrudgingly rode shotgun. Nonetheless, I was happy to get started. I had a duffle bag and an interview with Xerox Corporation in a few weeks, so it was a start. **A big shift was coming, in more ways than one. Remember the pivot.**

When we first arrived in New York City, it was intimidating and exciting at the same time. **It was a paradigm shift on many levels.** Various cultures mixed on every corner with people sharing the same buses and they could care less that my Manhattan Chapter was beginning. The subway never ceased to amaze me. Each trip was like a new adventure in people watching. I would actually venture to bet that someone from every culture around the world is represented in New York City. The food and the social life in New York City were unrivaled. It had something for everyone and was moving 24/7.

Amanda and I hit the ground running. With her dental school starting very soon and my job interview approaching, we were busy getting set up in our apartments and learning the basic ropes of where the grocery stores were and why the shopping carts were so small. I crashed on the couch of a friend from college who was very good to me. He was also in the city working, and he worked a lot so he enjoyed the company when he was off of work. **I felt bad that I didn't want to spend more time with him, but if you have ever been in real love, you know that you want to spend every moment possible with the person you love and that is where Amanda and I were in our relationship.**

The city was so new and fresh that we wanted to experience it all together. When the day of my job interview came, I was nervous. I didn't know what to expect. It was a long day. Every interview led to another interview, and by the end of the day, I had received an offer to work there. It was amazing. **I felt as if God had just said, "Now how obvious is that?" in regard to me questioning if I should try to stay in the city.** I walked into Amanda's apartment, and she said, "How did it go?" I don't think she or I ever expected that it was possible to be hired in one day, but we were both thrilled. The job gave her comfort about my desire to be happy at work and increase my chances to stay—and what man doesn't like to have work to do each day? It was go time. Amanda and I quickly developed a routine—her school and my work. **The grind of NYC was underway.** For our first year in New York, we pretty much kept to ourselves exploring every nook and cranny in the Big Apple.

Over the next four years in New York, we made some of the best friends from all over the world, **friends from all races and creeds. We had the pleasure of experiencing many of their cultures and enjoying food and tradition.**

From Koreans to Persians, people are largely the same. A few of our friends had family close by and we would even travel to family parties, so we had the pleasure of getting to know their parents and their homes. It just seemed easy for an ethnically diverse group to meet and eat and have fellowship in a city like New York. It truly was the most diverse city in the world. Amanda used to cringe because I would start a conversation with every cab driver we met. **I would get out of each cab ride a little more grateful and a little more proud of my country and the opportunity it provided for all races and creeds. We can't ever lose hope in the American Dream. It is available to all people at all times. Yes, I realize it can be very hard for people to get to the United States, but if they get here, they can have freedom and opportunity.**

I learned a lot about life living in New York City. I learned even more about myself. Initially, I had to climb "The Southern Wall." For the first six months of my New York City tenure, I absolutely hated the struggle and wanted to pull the parachute more than a few times. Amanda even tried to transfer back to dental school in South Carolina. She got in, but she would have to start over as a freshman. After watching her study so hard and all the early-rising mornings of studying, I couldn't bear the thought of her losing that year. Looking back, I am grateful transferring was not easy. I climbed "The Southern Wall" and got on the other side of six months. **It was like a new world was waiting there. I had built the wall in my mind.** Things did not have to be a certain way for them to be perfect in my mind. I saw what the city could offer. I am grateful for the lessons I learned. I cut my teeth in the Big Apple. **Frank Sinatra was right.** If you can make it there, you can make it anywhere. Thanks for the encouragement, Old Blue Eyes.

Now I don't expect your life experience to be my life experience, but I feel confident there are some common themes that can benefit us both. Your story is your story, just like my story is mine. **The main thing I have learned through nothing more than experiencing my own life and observing those experiencing life around me is that a life full of intention <u>but no action</u> only means nothing is ever going to get accomplished.** This shouldn't be a surprise to anyone, but <u>**unless a premium is placed on action,**</u> **things that are at rest usually tend to stay at rest—and that includes a behind staying seated on a coach.**

We all love to hear about plans and who is making them and who is going where when, but a plan for your life is a good idea. **I believe God made us all for his unique purposes.** I believe as much as he gave us free will and the ability to choose our actions and the path that we take in this life, God wants us to live for him on all levels. That sounds really weird and even scary when you think about it, but unless you think we have arrived at this moment in time merely by chance circumstances, **then God created your life for his purposes and by serving those purposes, you will be a joyful, peaceful, and successful person. You will be refining your desires in a way that will allow you and God to live in a perfect relationship that will not end.** Now to those who choose not to believe in God, I respect your freedom to choose and I appreciate you respecting my right to choose as well.

SHORT, SWEET, AND TO THE POINT—YOUR ELEVATOR PITCH

It's called an "Elevator Pitch." In the world of sales, it's when you tell a prospect why they should do business with you so succinctly that you could deliver your pitch in the time it takes to share an elevator ride. We all know it makes sense to be able to "pitch" our professional missions and values during business hours, **but can you articulate what you really believe about the purpose for your life, much less live it out, on a daily basis?** Can you express yourself effectively about how great this life experience is going to be for you and then live into that vision for yourself? **Today, can your express your M.O. (your modus operandi or mode of operation) and convince yourself, much less someone else, that you know what you are all about?**

Did you wake up today full of a clearly defined vision for your life, one that is bigger than yourself, while also feeling a sense of joy, inner peace, and actual balance? Do you have the desire to lead, equip, and inspire your spouse, children, immediate family, co-workers, and circle of influence? **On the most basic level, do you have a plan for your life for the rest of the time you have left to live?**

#H4E TEACHABLE MOMENT
Who Writes Your Definition of Success?

We need to start with success and understand how to define it. So let's do the "according to Webster's Dictionary" thing and reflect on the definition of success: "a person or thing that achieves desired aims or attains prosperity."

Well what does prosperity mean? Let's look that up too because success and prosperity seem to be related.

Prosperity is defined as "the state of being prosperous." Brilliant, but not really sure what that means either, so let's drill down on the word prosperous and we should have it all figured out. Prosperous means "successful in material terms; flourishing financially." OK, perfect. I knew it all along. Money and material things are the true definition of success. OK, let's go spread the good news with everyone about this so we can all examine how successful we are based on the amount of money and material things we have and then everything should easily fall into place. Turn in your score sheets when complete please.

Money and Material Things = Success, right?

CAPITAL WRONG! Not even close.

There isn't one definition for success. There may be one widely accepted definition of success across our American society, but success has many faces and the cool part of success **is that we each get to define it for ourselves.**

Repeat. Success is optional, but even more optional is us defining what success means to each one of us as unique individuals. Success is the achievement of your own predetermined worthwhile goals. **Your success will never be my success, and my success may not even be close to your definition of success either,** so let's go ahead and get this on the table. If we are going to operate under the belief that success is unique to each living, breathing human individual and the comparison game is broken, **you can finally be free from comparing yourself to others to determine if you are successful.**

It's like flipping your switch from scarcity to abundance, and there is much more juice on the abundance circuit than the scarcity link. If you can't wrap your mind around the difference, fear not, ye scarcity thinker—here is the difference.

A BAG OF BALLOONS

Have you ever bought a bag of balloons? You know what I mean, the one with all different shapes, sizes, and colors? Yellow, red, blue, green, pink, orange…round, long, wavy, and super skinny too. Balloon twisters go crazy for the super skinny one. The bag of balloons has a variety of shapes and sizes, colors, and strengths. If you blow up one of the round balloons and a super skinny balloon, they are not going to look the same. Each balloon in the bag has a different texture, size, and shape. If you study the balloons closely enough, even if you compare two with the same shape, you will find that they each have their own unique differences even if they look similar. Regardless of the color or shape of the balloon you pick out of the bag, you can blow up the balloon to its predesigned shape. Each balloon can have a different size and shape, but each balloon has a point of full capacity.

Rather than wishing we were a different shape or sized balloon, **wouldn't it be more fun and satisfying to simply focus on reaching our full capacity as a measure of success?** I think so. We all have unique talents and resources. **Examining what we already have in our possession is a great first step toward peace, joy, and successful contribution on planet earth.** The distractions are just as abundant as the opportunities and the noise around us is constant and endless, but only you can take charge of your life. The shape and size of your balloon may be beyond your control, **but only you can choose to fully inflate.**

YOUR SUCCESS BEGINS WITH A SUCCESSFUL THOUGHT LIFE

I am the most successful person I know because <u>I am the only person I know.</u> Think about THAT for a minute. You don't truly know anyone but yourself. You know your every thought, feeling, and potential reaction, and unless you lose control of your body, your thoughts become your actions. You may "know" other people, but you can't get in the head of anyone else to actually hear their train of thought. Your mind is the only mind that you can fully control. You can only assert, react, or respond to the rest of the world.

Our relationships with others are built on the character and behavior of other people and the individual and collective encounters we have with other people. "Success" is a moving target, and if anyone wants a fixed, predefined definition of success, then they are missing the point of this unique life experience that each of us gets to live. **Who has the right to call your life successful or unsuccessful anyway? No one… and I mean NO ONE.**

If someone deems your life successful or unsuccessful, they are really just basing this decision on their definition of success or some other model of success that they have seen or even experienced. Yes, we all know that a person strung out on drugs or under arrest or in the judicial process of heading to prison is not likely to be considered successful, but even those situations can be considered temporary. **Anyone can make a comeback at pretty much anytime, and everyone loves a comeback. <u>Be an underdog story.</u>**

It's hard to outrun your thought life. If you think constantly about eating a piece of cake and you really want a piece of cake, somewhere in your near future, you are going to have some variation of cake unless you change your train of thought by interrupting or changing the focus of your thoughts. Your closest friends don't know your innermost thoughts. We all have thoughts we would not share with anyone. Thankfully, others don't know what we are thinking because there may be times that we are ashamed of what we are thinking. Typically, those random thoughts are few and far between; however, we are always thinking whether for good or for bad, whether for idle or for productivity. Thoughts ultimately result in actions. **To have control over our thought life means that we can finally harness the power inside of each of us.**

So how do you control your thoughts? I wish it was an easy explanation, but it isn't, however the concept of **"garbage in, garbage out"** may be the best way to frame it. Poor thinking can lead to actions we regret later. It's kinda like desserts... I love desserts. Chocolate is an art to me, but I know that if I am planning a great, long distance ride on my bike, chocolate is not the fuel my body needs. Can I do it? Can I eat chocolate and go for a long ride and drink chocolate milk on the ride instead of packing water? Of course I can, but if things don't go as planned half way through the ride on a hot summer day and the sugar burns off and leaves me with an empty tank of energy with miles left, who can I blame at that point? The Government? Mr. Rogers? Clay Thompson (the official spokesperson of chocolate milk), who tells me the brown moo is the holy grail? Nope. I am fairly certain I can only blame myself. Man in the mirror time. Why, oh why, do we expect greatness from our actions when we have a junk food thought process and an empty calorie state of mind? Knowing and doing are two very distinctly, different things. How about this? What if we loved ourselves enough to put some good thoughts on the tip of our mind in the morning? What if we respected our minds, bodies and souls? Could we do cool stuff? Even if we don't do cool stuff, I am betting the odds of doing cool stuff would increase that day.

Do not spoil what you have by desiring what you have not; remember what you now have was once among the things you only hoped for.
—Epicurus

Here is an opportunity to capture some notes on your definition of success:

My Definition of Success is:

_____
_____
_____
_____
_____
_____

LOVE CONCEPT APPLIED - GOD HELP US BLESS EACH OTHER

We have all met a sourpuss before. How about someone that could care less? Grumpy airline worker, maybe? A fast-food worker with a beef (no pun intended)? The only problem with people is well...people. You will never stop someone from being rude or a jerk or even a flat-out criminal, but hey, mercy and grace aren't always free. Probably one of the most challenging things to do is kill someone with kindness. What is the alternative? Do you like to argue? Do you like to make your point? Do you have to get the last word? Sure, there are people out there like this, but when you experience people like this, you can rest assured that it is really just a behavior you are dealing with. Yes, there is a person behind it, but you have no way to understand what led that person up to your moment or encounter with them.

You have no idea how their day has been so far.

      A few months ago, I was eating in a Mexican restaurant in my town. I knew who the owner was, but I did not know him personally. While he was waiting on our table, I had the feeling that he was down. He was courteous and responsive to our table, but he was not overly jovial or animated. The next day I found out that the owner had lost his fifteen-year-old son the very day he waited on our table. His son had passed away in the hospital literally hours before he had to return to his business to operate it. Not only was my heart broken for the father because he had lost his only child, but my heart was broken for him that he had to return to his business the very same day instead of staying at the hospital to comfort himself and his grieving wife. Thank God that I did not make a negative judgment about the attitude and demeanor of my server. What would I have felt like if I had been the difficult patron?

      While I am certainly not a saint yet (there is no shame in striving for sainthood), I am grateful that I have adopted a "free pass" type of attitude with my interactions with other people when I know that I will most likely never ever see them again in my entire lifetime. How many people do you remember meeting once and you are fairly confident that you will never ever see them again? What was that one interaction like? Were you full of grace or full of mace? Ever cleared customs in a foreign country while traveling? Any chance you will see that customs officer again? How about the bouncer who checked your identification the one time you visited your friend in Kansas? How about the cashier who checked you out when you were passing through the interstate convenience store? Some interactions last only seconds, but the way we choose to conduct ourselves really can make it a blessing or a curse.

      I will be the first one to admit that it is hard to invest love and continual support even to the people with whom we have the closest relationships, so we all know how difficult it is to give our best to each interaction in this life, especially when we have so many **disposable encounters.** Many cultures can read your eyes. Are your eyes kind? Do you have a smile or a pleasant expression for others? Choose to be a blessing to others. It is a choice.

POSITIVE AFFIRMATION STATION

I used to think "positive affirmation" was all smoke and mirrors. Self-affirmation through the selection or creation of positive statements about myself just seemed odd. How could the repeating of positive statements truly result in positive actions taking place all around me? **There is great power in the words that we chose to use.** If you are a parent or have ever had a pet, how often did you have to remind the child or pet to remember the correct behavior you wanted to see? It most likely took a few times for you to remind the child or pet to do the desired result. With consistency of your desires and reinforcement of your expectations, you likely made progress until a new habit pattern was finally established. Our minds can also be trained to behave in such a way.

Our minds can be taught to believe in the better side of life. Our minds can be renewed with hope and whether we understand the subconscious mind or not, we can have ownership of the way we choose to think. **Our mind is a muscle**—however how powerfully do we really think? Has your mind ever wandered? Have you ever realized that you had allowed a random thought to take your mind in a direction that was totally unproductive? You have full control over your mind. It is probably the only thing that you can control.

The power of free thought is an amazing realization. Choose to think in a way that can lead you toward the person that you want to become. Our thoughts become us, so make sure you are staying aware of how you think.

Your thoughts become words, and words become actions. A lazy thought process can be dangerous.

Here are some examples of affirmations that I use on a daily basis:

1. I was born to Lead, Equip, and Inspire others in all areas of my life.

2. The #Hustle4Ever Way of Life prioritizes Faith, Family, Fitness, Business, and CommUnity.

3. As long as I am ethical and moral in my conduct and keep the promises that I have made **then I don't care what other people think of me.**

You can create your own affirmations that resonate with you. Affirmations can come in all shapes and sizes. They can be spiritual statements, family goals or even business related. You can switch them up or repeat the same statements for the rest of your life, but it is important that you spend some quality time putting together the best affirmations for your life. This is an exercise that you want to take seriously because it will help shape your new thought life.

#H4E TEACHABLE MOMENT
Quadruple Threat Position

For decades, people have been talking about "Triple Threat" Position. I am all about "Quadruple Threat" Position. And what is the most important part on and off the court before you dribble, pass or shoot? It is to think about what is the best option. An impulsive dribbler can easily dribble into trouble. A quick shooter can easily become a ball hog and a lazy passer can become a turnover king, but to think before you act… that is making Magic a happy man. Sometimes you can't see it until you can see it, but a thinking man or woman increases the chances what they think might happen, might actually happen.

A PREMIUM MUST BE PLACED ON ACTION

Thought or intention without action is really just a pipe dream. Now, I am all for dreaming, but at some point (sooner rather than later) the person who takes action is more likely to succeed even if the actions initially result in multiple failures. Failure is a teacher, but at least we actually tried our hand at ringing the bell of full potential realization.

How many times have you heard that someone has "so much potential"? Maybe you have said that about someone you know or maybe you have been the person who was underperforming or plain goofing off. **Perspective and self- awareness are gifts.** So often we are too close to ourselves. Have you ever felt as if your reflection looked differently in certain mirrors and lighting than other mirrors? Sure you have. Think about the fair when you were growing up. There was the mirror that made you look stretched out and skinny and then the mirror that made you look like a short, squatty version of yourself. How about staying in hotels and looking better in one mirror at one hotel than in a different hotel mirror? Are the mirrors and the lighting different? Sure they are, but maybe that's not what's making the difference. Maybe it is just the way you feel about yourself in that moment in time.

Our self-esteem and self-love can wax and wane just like our hairstyle can change over the years, hopefully for the better in both cases, but we have all seen a lot of mullets (and the word on the street is that they are making a comeback). Mirrors are easy to change or even remove, but **every now and then, we need to take a hard look in the mirror, smell our own breath, and take inventory of our lives.** What are we living for? What time do we have on our hands and what can we do with it? What talents do we have—and not just the talents we think we have but **the talents that have been affirmed again and again by those that know us best?** What types of resources do you have? Do you have money? Do you have access to certain people or places? How will you use this power or persuasion? Long story short: you are you and no one else is. Yes, birds of a feather flock together, but you still have your place on the wire in the grand scheme of life. Even if you don't know what your place is today at this given moment, **you have a responsibility not to bury your talents.** The very next corner could be your break…your epiphany…your purpose finally realized. And that, my friend, is going to be pure joy. Joy like it was meant for you because it was. So let's hustle to get there.

#H4E TEACHABLE MOMENT
Open Up to Affirmations

When people tell you that you do something well or that you "should" be this or be that… do you contemplate it? It is all to easy to see ourselves with limiting views. When people tell you they perceive you to be good at something, then let your ears perk up. We all know that from the outside looking in, things can look differently. Other people's comments are profoundly helpful when we are in a period of discernment. Accept affirmations. They are clues you can use.

POWER LIFT YOUR BRAIN

Hey, you must work out, right? Well, I was talking to your brain. I love the fact that my mind is a muscle. My brain is waiting on me to feed it with good thoughts and affirmations. It wants to work. Leave it idle a brain is just like water, the thought quality trickles downhill quickly.

Your brain is a good brain, and it wants to do BIG things for you and for the world around you. **When was the last time you just sat around to think?** The scary part is that sometimes we get lost in the most unproductive thought— the "Am I worthy?" train of thought. Listen, you aren't being honest with yourself if you haven't had some level of doubt at some point in your life and no one likes a liar, bless your heart (and the Southern Ladies chuckle).

#H4E TEACHABLE MOMENT
No Cute Subtitles Here. Suicidal Thinkers Take Action.

Have you ever been shocked when you heard about someone you know committing suicide? Wow. There is never any way to prepare for that sad news, but if you don't think mental illness is out there, then you need to pay attention a little more. Unfortunately, I have experienced the painful losses of suicide. My grandfather committed suicide as well as one of my best friends. The wake is wide, and I would be lying to you if I told you that the wake ever goes away, not just for the immediate family, but for the network of friends and acquaintances. **The collateral damage of suicide is too massive to comprehend or even begin to explain.** We can only hope to move on by taking our minds off of the situation, and yes, time does start to heal our wounds or at least dull the shock of the initial news and funeral, but scars will always remain and that is just the truth. Some scars look better than others, but **scars are scars.** They become a part of you. From family members to friends or acquaintances, I have seen all sides of suicide. It's ugly, so if you have thoughts of killing yourself, trust me and admit you have a problem and call someone or a hotline right now and tell them you need help. There is no shame in admitting you need counseling or therapy or even medication to help you through difficult times of poor thinking and your confidentiality will be protected by law.

Poor thinking today does not have to be poor thinking forever. Just like we get the flu and think we are going to die but then get better, we will get better at some point. Quitting, however, is going to burn a lot of folks for a long, long time. There is zero shame in coping with mental illness. It is actually quite the contrary. It takes one brave person to admit they have problems with their thought life. **Therapy works,** and there are many places to get started. Check out my resource section in the back of the book to take the first step.

PEOPLE WATCHING STARTS IN THE MIRROR

Do you care enough to observe? Reflect? I would venture to guess that we all like to people watch. Watching people behave is fascinating. We have all witnessed impressive behavior and certainly we have all seen poor behavior. Observation and examination go hand in hand. Too often we condemn or judge others because **we tend to believe that if we were put in a similar situation (regardless of what type of situation it is—good or bad), that we would behave flawlessly.**

We have all heard of the "peanut gallery" or "armchair quarterback." The peanut gallery and the armchair are typically where critics live. You don't have to be famous to have critics. Critics can be your spouse, children, friends, co- workers, sports teammates, or even strangers on a bus. **You, YES YOU, yourself could also be your own critic,** which is extremely dangerous.

I mentioned that **self-awareness is a true gift,** and I mean it. To know that your breath smells after a spicy lunch or that you have body odor because you have been working in the yard—these are simple examples of self- awareness. Keep going…it does not have to end there. Self-awareness of how we walk, talk, and listen can truly change our lives for the better. Do you sabotage your nutrition with certain binges? Do you smile at someone and tell them how nice they look and go home and talk smack about their outfit? Do you go to church but then contradict everything you proclaim to believe all week long at work? Do you know it is wrong to flirt with a married man yet you secretly love the attention? **Psst, STOP!**

Have you ever taken a **simple inventory of your life?** I encourage you to do so and simply put a line down the middle of a piece of paper. On the left, start writing down the blessings and good things in your life. **Don't rush to get to the negative side—really dig in and think about all that you have to be grateful for.** Little things matter too, such as appreciating the fact that you can use your own hands to feed and bathe yourself, or even breathe on your own— real fundamental stuff that we often overlook.

So fill up your grateful side (I call it "BLEST"), and then when you turn your focus to the right side of the paper for the things that you will be tempted to call "negatives," change the title of the column to "Areas I Will Improve" or "Anti-Sabotage". Start jotting them down. "Lose 20 pounds," next, "Stop cursing," next, "Fix my marriage," next, "Get back to church," and so on and so on. Once you have completed the list, you may need to put it away and go do something else for a while and then come back to it. If you feel inspired or even depressed by the list and want to keep working on it, I won't stop you, but really examine the "Areas I Will Improve" AKA "No MORE SELF-SABOTAGE!" side and start prioritizing which areas you would really like to see change first.

Think about why you have these items on your list and how they got on the list in the first place. The reality is that your behaviors in the past or the past behaviors of other people of influence in your life put those written words on that page. For example, maybe "stop cursing" is on your list. **Where did you learn that behavior? Trace it back.** You have decided to curse on some level, so examine why you allowed cursing to happen. I tell my kids all the time that cursing is proof that you have a lack of vocabulary, but every now and again, I let some curse words fly, for emphasis more than anything. I actually hate that about myself, so I make a concerted effort to control it. Maybe you do the same thing or maybe you had a mother who was always cursing and you picked up an unattractive quality. Go through each item on your "Areas I Will Improve" list.

Examine it and start suggesting to yourself how you will **IMMEDIATELY change it.** If you can't see a way to make an immediate change, then you need to engage the proper counselor, priest, or therapist to start making your comeback.

Decide to reach out IMMEDIATELY and slay the list. When in doubt, start with a priest or pastor. Understand that they are sitting on so many resources that a first conversation will be free and can get you on a more solid path of progress. If you don't have a current church, go to the last church you attended and seek that priest or pastor, even if it was years ago. If you have moved away from that area, seek a church of the same denomination you were raised in if you are more comfortable with that. If you didn't go to church growing up, then go to the closest Catholic Church. **The Catholic Church has one of the largest networks of charity resources and a heart to serve people when they are ready to turn their pain into power.** The Catholic Church will never be perfect because humans are involved, but the network of every day Samaritans is real.

Don't let a past negative connotation keep you from starting your journey because that is unfortunately ignorance holding you back from a breakthrough. No church is perfect just like no person is perfect, but if you spend some time searching around any church, at some point, you are going to find the right person in a particular church that truly has the desire to help.

IT AIN'T ABOUT ME…YET

Where were you born? Tell me about it. Wow, that is interesting, and then what happened? What is your story?

We all have a story. Sometimes we like certain movies and sometimes we think some movies are the worst, but those movies still exist and they can't be undone even if they went straight to video and the actor didn't want you to know. Your life is like a movie that plays from start to finish, and I will guarantee you there aren't any intermissions, cuts, or reshoots. It is one continuous journey, and the plot can be an Oscar winner or some B-roll on the cutting-room floor. All that really matters is that when you rewind your movie and look back on the highlights at the end of your life, you can feel as if you really went for it, that you really attempted to "ring the bell" of your full potential. I mean a deep, solid ring that lets the whole world know that this bell, yeah, it just got rung.

So how will you judge your movie? How will you determine if you fulfilled your life's purpose? **I will venture to say that your level of success is going to be determined by your definition of success and the people who are going to cry at your funeral. Wait, rewind. I will venture to say that your level of success is going to be determined by your definition of success and the people who are going to cry at your funeral.** I won't make you read that a third time, but let me just draw your attention to the fact that this concept is a **GAME CHANGER THAT WILL QUICKLY PUT YOUR PRIORITY PEOPLE ON ONE HAND—OR MAYBE TWO IF YOU HAVE A BIG FAMILY OR ALREADY UNDERSTAND THE POWER OF YOUR POSITIVE INFLUENCE.**

Your story may not be all that exciting to the whole world. Just think of all the people that have no idea that your life is going on right now and quite honestly could care less even if they did. Depressing, I know, BUT, your story is going to count to a pretty strong circle of influence that typically goes like this: your mom and dad, your spouse, your children, your co-workers, your "dailies" (people you see pretty frequently), and then the rest of the population pretty much falls off the cliff in the level of concern or care they have about you. I know, cold right? Well, I didn't come here to toot your horn. I came here to make it blow—and not like the trumpet in the attic that Uncle Charlie played one time before he quit and you thought it would be a cool Halloween prop. **This story that I refer to is real. It is the story of your life.**

You are the only main character. Life only lives from your perspective. We can't get hung up on anyone else's perspective of happiness except our own, but we must discover happy and discover joy to know if we are even getting close to living it. **Happy does not have to be elusive.** You are letting happiness elude you. Why would you ever accept happiness eluding you? **Happiness works for you, you don't work for Happy.** Get it? See what happens to Happy if he shows up late and you will let Happy know who the boss is. Happy will be sorry for trying to think he or she is the boss of me. No sir. **I am the boss of Happy.**

Do you think your story is a good one or does it pretty much stink? Take a deep breath because I am about to give you some truth and you may need to take a seat so you can really drink this one in. **If your story ain't all that great, you are making it stink.** Your story will probably continue to struggle as well if you let it keep drowning. **Don't do that anymore.** Your story is being written. Right now at this very moment, your story is being written just as sure as I am writing this book and you are reading it. **Your story is going to go down in history.** It may only go down in the history of your family tree, but make it seriously go down with so much funky flavor that you become the legend that you know God wants you to be. Introvert or extrovert, it doesn't matter, your style is your style, but your life is a lamp and light to the world. Don't hide it under a bush where the light is hidden away from the world. Put the lamp on the lampstand and let it shine baby!

JOY + LOVE = PEACE.
BOOM! LOVE FINALLY EXPLAINED

Simple statement. Joy inside with love expressed outside can set you up for a peaceful life. World peace is beyond a cliché these days because I am not too sure any of us believe deep down in our souls that it can happen in our lifetimes, but we can't stop trying. Ultimately, world peace or personal peace can only happen when human beings, as individuals, start really living it. Individuals create momentum, and if enough start pushing peace, we can get there as humankind. **The peace starts within. If you don't master personal peace, local, state, national or world peace will never even take a breath of hope.**

If you can't honestly say that you have a joyful life each day, then we need to start there. It is somewhat like a troubleshooting guide. You know the kind that say if you have part A then skip to step 2, if you don't have part A then do step 1? If you don't have joy **authentically** in your heart today, then we will need to skip to love and start there. This is going to sound crazy, especially if you are depressed,

but expressing love to the world in the form of every living thing you come in contact with is the only way to break the cycle of depression and lack of joy. What you put out will come back to you. It is that simple.

Whether you read The Five Love Languages by Gary Chapman or The Four Loves by C. S. Lewis, love is better lived out when it is better understood and even explained to children properly at an early age. We throw around the word "love" like it means nothing, but it means so much. It is so deep that you can't even imagine touching the bottom. Let's take a moment to really understand love and how you can properly express it. Many men and women over the years have put the wrong expression of love in the wrong love bucket, ruining relationships and feelings only to sour the individuals involved in the process.

I was on a family trip in London with some good friends. We were having a blast as we finished up our dinner at a dessert house. The adults were sitting at one table, and the children were sitting the next table over. As our married friends gave each other a sweet kiss while the adults were laughing, the couple's daughter came over and somewhat aggressively stopped her parents from any romantic gestures. She did this twice. I think we all knew why. Often children (and even adults) don't understand that love is like a diamond. It has many facets and beautiful angles that allow God's love to shine in so many directions. I asked the little girl if I could explain love to her. She nodded her head up and down (still somewhat in a pout), and I explained to her that love has many faces and that love is a beautiful thing. You see, **complete love is our goal.** Complete love has a time and a place and a season for all human beings. We so easily think of love only in the sexual and physical sense. That is the easiest one to confuse because of our media outlets today and because whoever or however we learned about physical love, most likely didn't perfectly complete the explanation. While my explanation was brief and certainly age appropriate, the little girl had her "a-ha moment." She smiled and seemed pleased to understand that Mom and Dad kissing was an expression of their love that now affirmed the little girl's existence and inclusion rather than competed with her feeling of "how do I fit in here and do they love each other more than they love me?" The parents were pleased as well. I hope they now don't ever have to hide thier kisses away again. Upon first edit of this book, I was advised to remove a summary explanation of love to expand on what happened in London. At first, it seemed like a good idea. Maybe the simple example of the little girl was enough to explain love, but the more I saw the strikethrough of the explanation of love in the book draft, the more I realized that this is the crux of the problem, we don't fully understand love and we certainly don't want to invest any time grinding out complete love in our lives. It's a shame that we don't understand self-love and the love of others. Many problems could fade away if we understood the simple explanation of love so let me draw up a play for you to take away and use:

#H4E TEACHABLE MOMENT – This is one of the most important lessons...
THE LOVE SPECTRUM =

Philautia - Agape - Philia – Ludus - Eros – Storge - Pragma

Heart__P_____A_____P_____L_____E_____S_____P___Heart

(Greek Root Words and according to Psychology Today)

1) **Philautia** is self-love, which can be healthy or unhealthy.

2) **Agape** is universal love, such as the love for strangers, nature, or God.

3) **Philia** are friendships founded on goodness are associated not only with mutual benefit but also with companionship, dependability, and trust.

4) **Ludus** relationships are casual, undemanding, and uncomplicated but, for all that, can be very long-lasting. Ludus works best when both parties are mature and self-sufficient. Flirting is a good way to summarize Ludus.

5) **Eros** is passionate love and is the type most akin to our modern construct of romantic love.

6) **Storge** or familial love, is a kind of philia pertaining to the love between parents and their children.

7) **Pragma** is a kind of practical love founded on reason or duty and one's longer-term interests. Romantic love is put on the back burner here. Common goals or shared goals are more important.

Love has a progression and there is nothing wrong with "Love" being different for different relationships in your life. Here are some important steps to understand and apply love in your life:

1) Love Yourself = Philautia

2) Respect other human life, even if they are strangers = Agape

3) When a relationship grows into a friendship with someone, be a good friend = Philia

4) If you think you might have romantic feelings for someone, test those feelings responsibly with words and maturity first and understand this is a delicate step in a relationship so think before you act. At this phase, you may not be ready to be exclusive and you should be honest about that = Ludus

5) Once you have committed to an exclusive relationship, you should honor it and support the other person on every level that is healthy for both you and your significant other. If you are old enough and committed enough to get engaged, please seek pre-marital counseling. There is so much more to this than you can even imagine = Eros

6) If you are blessed with children, love them deeply and keep loving your partner regardless of how busy or stressed your life might become. Children are a physical manifestation of two people's love = Storge

7) Love all your relationships appropriately and understand that you can have a different "love" relationship with all people in your life and that is okay = Pragma

As long as you care enough to understand love and know where the appropriate boundaries of love are, you will truly live out a loving life for yourself and others. You may move back and forth on the spectrum and relationships have the ability to change, some for the better, some not. Although the "Spectrum" or "Journey" of Love is spelled out in general above, think about it on an every day level. **You must love yourself and never feel guilty for loving yourself.** This is easier said than done. I am a confident man, but we all have moments of self-doubt, fear of failure or wonder how worthy we really are on some level. They may be quick flashes of doubt, but some may really struggle to have belief in themselves and wonder if they should keep trying. Well I say keep trying and definitely keep building up your self-love, self worth and self respect. You don't have to put yourself up in the Ritz every night to love yourself… you can simply acknowledge that you have strengths and good qualities and those outweigh the weaknesses (we all have weaknesses so let's be real, peeps.)

Let's test the spectrum with a real life example and assume that the relationship is not a family member because that is a whole other ball of wax. No matter your age, when you meet someone new, you size them up and try to find common ground. Whether extrovert or introvert, sometimes it takes a very long time and sometimes it seems like you don't have any common ground at all. And guess what, you might not have any common ground. As long as you love yourself and you respect yourself, you can easily walk away from the other person you have met and decide that you will wish them well on their journey of life as they go figure things out for themselves, but you don't necessarily need to spend any more time with that person. Maybe your paths will cross again in the future and things will be different. Maybe they won't. Either way, move on. So you only made it to "Step 2" (remember Agape?) with that person. Hey, that's okay. That's just one person in this world. You have made it to other steps with your good friends… friends that appreciate you and care about you. Yes, you made it to "Step 3" (remember Philia?) with those folks. Fantastic. When you find your partner for life, you may end up at "Step 6" (catch my drift by now I hope?) with children and spend the rest of your lives together. Love is awesome and often cheapened and certainly misunderstood. **Be Love Smart,** it's a wonderful thing.

Family relationships don't always play by the "Love Spectrum" rules. Respect and tolerance can often bully true love communication. Fairness can be hard to find in difficult family relationships. It is going to be case by case and how your family functioned before you were born into it, but despite how it is, that doesn't mean that is how it has to exist. Communication and change is very hard, but with courage and grace, **any family** can be restored or at least a future legacy can be changed for the better.

LOVE WAS MEANT TO BEAR FRUIT

The **Fruit of the Holy Spirit** is a biblical teaching that sums up nine attributes of a person or community living in accord with the Holy Spirit according to the Epistle to the Galatians: "But the fruit of the Spirit is **love, joy, peace, patience, kindness, goodness, faithfulness, gentleness, and self- control."** If you project out to the world and to the people you have relationships with any of the fruits of the spirit, your life can only get better. If you withhold these fruits or even seek to harm those around you, you are really only harming yourself (and your fruit spoils and starts to stink and stinks you up with it… think banana peel). You may not see it for years, but this is the simple reality of people who choose to be negative in this life. They never were taught love, so they were left only with room for weeds and non-fruit-bearing plants to grow. Love can grow at any moment, but it can take years to help someone see this.

LOVE CONCEPT APPLIED - GOD HELP US BLESS THE ELDERLY

They are slow, sometimes smell, and should have their driver's licenses revoked. It's time for them to step down, head off to pasture, and stop telling us about the good ole days (because they didn't do anything to keep America free or anything small like that). The only problem with this attitude is that we are talking about ourselves. I have looked into this, and there is no way out of this aging game. Have you ever imagined yourself as an eighty-year-old? Push the thought back and cage it away as if that will make it just a myth. It's hard to imagine my wife as an eighty-year-old or my children as senior citizens, but unless something changes, this is a reality that is coming as surely as I write at this very moment.

Pushing reality away will not change it. I am afraid to look at the health and beauty spending in the United States. I can only imagine the number, and it is probably ten times more than we would guess anyway. I am all about taking care of myself. I believe in annual physicals, eye exams, hearing tests, and preventative checks. That said, there is only so much I can do to optimize my body without freezing it, which evidently is now a thing. **I believe that each season of life is beautiful.** Life is an experience that has plenty of changes. How beautiful is it to see a toddler bump her head only to watch her shake it off and even forget it happened twenty seconds later, while the same bump could literally end an elderly woman. We have amazing strength and resilience in our youth. As we age, we don't always get to control how much balance we will have or if we will still be able to dress ourselves.

The way we treat elderly people says a lot about belief in human dignity. Yes, they ask a lot of questions in the post office line and maybe even straddle the parking lot line, but they used to run full speed, move and shake at work, and most likely got slapped in the mouth a few times defending this country. We can learn so much from our elders. Yes, some lived life well and some didn't do so hot, but there is a level of respect that we need to give the elderly we encounter each day. It's just the right thing to do. Extend a hand, open a door, tell them they look nice today. If you think some of the wisest people on the planet like the fact that they are sitting in retirement homes or in and out of hospitals and doctor's offices, you couldn't be more wrong. Honor the elderly and make each encounter special for them. If you don't, please don't be surprised when it's your turn to rock the blue hair (if you have hair) later in life and people scoff right back at you. You will get what you give so slow down and love on some old people, whether you are related to them or not. That is just good living.

SEASONS OF LIFE

If you have ever heard your mother, father, or spouse say that they miss it when the children were small, then you can relate to how fast time flies by. No one believes the cliché of "you won't believe how fast it goes by" until you start to experience it yourself. While I do get a little teary-eyed when I see video of my children as babies and toddlers, I have experience with each season of life. Just like the weather seasons, we go through new seasons of life. When your child starts walking. When your child goes to college. When your parents die. When you grow old yourself. Time marches on, and it can never be put back on the clock. That is a reality we all know, but very seldom do we stop to appreciate this reality. It can be overwhelming to really let this sink in.

Time stops for no man, woman or child. It is hard to look in the mirror and see an older version of yourself, especially remembering that when you were younger you couldn't wait to grow up. Then when you get there, you wish time would slow down and even rewind. **Can you appreciate today?** I don't mean this year or your short-term plans, but I mean today. Can you appreciate the last breath you took without thinking about it five seconds ago? There are so many seasons to this life experience than we ever care to reflect upon. How many regrets will there be at the end of our lives? Hard to imagine that we haven't missed a few opportunities here and there, even if to take back some simple words that came out the wrong way.

We have a warped sense of perspective at times, maybe for the better. We subconsciously know there is a countdown occurring, but if we thought about the countdown all the time, we could never enjoy the present. A daily gratitude perspective really can change your life for the better. Otherwise you miss what is before you. Let's all strive to honor the seasons of life and respect the seasons in the lives of others. Milestones are never a burden if we honor them the right way.

DOES THIS BOOK EVER END?

When we study history books as children, we learn valuable lessons from the great men and women and even children that lived before us. Think of a great documentary that you have seen. Maybe even an Oscar winning story of someone's life. The story always seems complete in the movies. No matter if they were a hero, an underdog or even the villain. One way or the other, the story seems complete. It has a start, a middle and an end. Literary classes are built around this framework, but what happens if your story is still being written? What if we have a game in progess and the outcomes are still being determined? It's not so clean that way is it? My story…your story…these stories are still being written. As much as I talk about hitting the pause button to reflect, there really isn't a pause button at all now is there? The second that just dripped off the clock isn't ever coming back. It is long gone by now. Why are we chosing to play small? Aren't we all living well below our full potential? What makes a child grow into a "Captain of Industry" or a "Woman on the Rise"? Don't look to me for answers, I am just the one typing in the letters, you are the once choosing to write the story. Have you embraced yours? Do you have a pencil with an eraser? Let's sharpen it and start over now.

The RALLY

There comes a point in time when a spark has to ignite. When the time to change is either going to happen or not. A relationship needs to change or a family needs to make a change or a business is going to make a change. Maybe you, yourself, are going to make a change whether it's diet, job, or even hairstyle.

There has to be a moment of ignition that must take place for a change to happen. So how do you make that moment take place? How do you make the change start to occur if you know you have a long journey ahead of you?

You have to take the first step. As cliché as it sounds, you must take action. You can write all of the self-affirming thoughts you want on a piece of paper, but unless you're willing to take action, nothing is ever going to occur. Intentions are lifeless until action steps occur.

I call for the rally and I am screaming for it at the top of my lungs. I call for legacies to be established beginning with you and me. The culture of change must start somewhere. If you've ever played a sport and have been down at halftime and your coach gave you a rousing speech of encouragement (whether or not he or she was throwing chairs across the room), did it do something for you? Did it ignite the fire or create a spark and did you rally? Or did you go out there for the second part of the game and just continue to stink? **Failure is an option. Failure has a lot to teach us, but you can never willingly agree to go out like a punk. It is okay to rally. Give yourself permission to be great. Be exceptional. Be you.**

THE LAST #H4E TEACHABLE MOMENT IN THIS BOOK

THE HARD PIVOT

Today, I find myself as a 44-year-old man with deep faith and hope for eternal life, a solid family life, a strong body and good health habits along with successful businesses that are trending upwards and love for my community and fellow human beings, whether they look like me or not. I can sincerely say that the above sentence isn't merely a positive affirmation statement, but rather a reality. I am BLEST (Sorry Mom, it's a play on words, yes, I know it should be "Blessed"). It took work and it took effort (more effort than I thought it would take), but it happened and I want each man, woman and child to experience the same thing from the alleys of Ho Chi Minh to the La Jolla Coast. Everyone wants to advertise the "best life", but it is a lot harder to actually go get it, but not as hard as you might think it to be. It starts with a firm reality check and Quadruple Threat Position and certainly a spirit of hustle. Once you see where you are, once you take a personal inventory of your life and actually take the time to hit the pause button, you can **MAKE YOUR HARD PIVOT.** I have the gift of observation and reflection and it is time for you to appreciate the same thing. You are where you chose to be and it is that simple. Every human life has circumstances, but regardless of career, country or religion, there are stories on this planet that prove that someone made it. Someone went higher. Someone just like you rang the bell, tipped the scales and broke the mold. Limitations broken, stereotypes tuned out, shots scored and prayers answered. What will it take for you to pivot? Will it be the right time and place tomorrow? Why not now? Why not today. This is the day. The time is now. Make your pivot… and may you #Hustle4Ever..

#Hustle4Ever | define your success

fingerprint

How to write your OWN Definition of Success and Win at Life

by David Seay

HACK PACK™

#Hustle4Ever™ and #Hustle4Ever Fingerprint™. ALL RIGHTS RESERVED.

#Hustle4Ever

define your success

_____ Way of Life by _____

My Theme is _____

Success is a daily habit, not a destination. Map out goals that you want to accomplish and then pursue them with reckless abandon, defining your own success and investing in yourself your entire life. The comparison model is broken so don't even play that game, but enjoy the journey to get your best life. God has a plan and a purpose for you at each season of your life. Don't believe anything other than that. You reap what you sow. Reap well.

#Faith4Ever

_____

_____

_____

_____

#Family4Ever and #Friends4Ever:

_____

_____

_____

_____

#Fitness4Ever and #Sports4Ever:

_____

_____

_____

_____

#Academics+Career+HustleSkills/CommUnity4Ever:

_____

_____

_____

_____

#My Definition of Success is

_____

_____

_____

_____

#Hustle4Ever™ by Coach Seay. All Rights Reserved. Please feel free to reproduce and share with this line included.

#Hustle4Ever

define your success

fingerprint

#Family4Ever Mission - To Make Your Family Awesome or Even More Awesome on a Daily Basis

Model A Great Example of a Family That Inspires You:

Example:
The Holy Family

Your Example:
_____

Positive Way to Start Your Day:

Example:
Daily Gratitude – Count your blessings, no matter how small like your heartbeat or even the ability to smile.

Your Example:
_____

Pray for others – Pull for your brothers and sisters, parents and other people around you. God has plenty for everyone. Abundance is a mindset.

Your Example:
_____

A Family Mission Statement must be timeless and worthy to pass onto the next generation.

> The Seay Family likes to live, learn, love and have fun adventures while spending quality time together all focused on Faith, Family, Fitness, Business and Community Contribution. Unconditional Love lives in our home. This is our legacy. We lead, equip and inspire.

Principles:

To be who we are
To have harmony
To learn from our mistakes
To leave things better than we found them
To listen and seek to understand one another
To maintain self control and find a peaceful way
To respect others and not interrupt
We don't say "can't" because we can

Understand the Value behind all the talks and the lessons provided by parents. You have to choose to see the value in each lesson.
Write Your Family4Ever Mission Statement, then LIVE IT!
A Family Mission Statement must be timeless and worthy to pass onto the next generation.

_____
_____
_____
_____
_____

Your Principles (The Character of Your Family):

_____
_____
_____
_____
_____

The #Family4Ever Story

If you haven't see the #Family4Ever Video, please take a moment to watch it.

"I invest my life in the people that are going to cry at my funeral."
- Dan Mortimer

#Fitness4Ever "MINDMAP" by Coach Seay

THE HEALTH & NUTRITION THINKING THAT CHANGES LIVES™

Why Do We Do What We Do?

If we do not control our habits, our habits will begin to control us and ultimately define us. Habits should work for us, not the other way around.

How often do you examine your fitness and health goals in relation to your daily exercise and nutritional decisions to fairly access if your habits are positive or negative? Are your habits growing you or decaying you?

TODAY IS THE DAY to claim good habits and connect your actions to your desired result.

1) Think BIG! (Begin In Gratitude)

I AM grateful for _____

(Example: I AM grateful for the ability to freely move my body and feed myself.)

2) Visualize Your Success

Claim, affirm and believe a vision of how you are going to look and feel when you have obtained eating habits, a fitness routine and the body image that you desire.

WRITE IT OUT IN A POSITIVE TONE AND SENTENCE:
_____
_____

(Example: I AM proud of my physical transformation and the new found strength and energy I feel to move with excitement today and serve the people around me that I love and appreciate.)

3) Literally See Your Success With The Use Of An Image

Find an image of the desired body type that you will accomplish. You can use a picture from a magazine or a past image of yourself when you were most proud of your body. Just make sure it is a positive picture with the person doing a positive activity like running, walking, laughing or walking on the beach.

CUT AND GLUE YOUR IMAGE HERE:

> GLUE YOUR IMAGE HERE. TYPE IN "Healthy Body Images" in your search engine and select "images" once the results return and look for a good picture that represents where you want to go. Then, insert that image here simply by printing it, cutting it to the size of this box and use glue or tape to put it over this text. Reference this image often even if you hang this sheet on your wall or put it in your gym bag. Look at it before, during or after your work out or hang it anywhere that can help you avoid sabotage (Ex. in the kitchen).

(Example: I have upgraded my image over the years. I have used pictures I have found from the internet and I typically just use a picture with no head or face so that I increase my chances that I envision myself accomplishing the results I want to obtain.)

4) Express WHY you desire your improved health and body

When you know why you are doing something and you recall the motivation behind your actions, you use certainty to push yourself past your fears and weak moments when self-sabotage is most likely. Define and recall your reason "WHY".

WHY are you accomplishing better health/nutritional habits for your mind and body?
___
___
___

(Example: I KNOW that I deserve to feel comfortable in my own skin and that I deserve to be healthy and strong so that I can reach my personal and professional dreams and say YES to all the good things life has to offer me. I was created to be great and I will not accept being mediocre anymore. I will become the best version of myself no matter what! I EXPECT an improved life now and am CERTAIN that it is happening to me. I am worthy to receive it!)

My WHY Theme is _____

(Example: A Theme is a word or tagline that gives you quick motivation. My WHY Theme is "Execution", which reminds me that a life with only intention and not specific action steps is just talk and not walk.)

#Fitness4Ever GOALS - Name your specific goals through affirmative statements:
(Example: I AM 15 pounds lighter by the end of this year and walk/run 10 minutes more each day.)
___
___
___
___
___
___

My Definition of #Fitness4Ever Success is:
(Example: If you look back on your fitness and health efforts one year from today, what would you have accomplished to consider yourself successful? Define your OWN success and then go get it!)

It is one year from today and my #Fitness4Ever SUCCESS looks like this:
___
___
___
___
___
___

> You have a choice to make. Choose Health, Vigor and Energy for Life. Exhaustion, Low Self Esteem and Poor Body Image are the results if you do nothing. Run away from this pain. Once you breakthrough the mediocrity of your past, you will cherish your exercise and nutrition. You will crave this powerful part of your daily life. Each day will be filled with passion for life!
> **YOU MUST BELIEVE IN YOUR #FITNESS4EVER AND STARTOW!**

#Fitness4Ever Calendar

"REBOOT HABIT CALENDAR" by Coach Seay

1ST 23 DAYS

Changing Habits - Psychology

Science has shown us that if you can change a habit for 23 consecutive days, you can remap a NEGATIVE behavior to a desired behavior. Repeat the 23-day mental exercise for two additional periods of 23 days and you can close the door on going back to a bad habit or behavior. Self-Sabotage is important to avoid during a process of rewiring your choices and habits and an elevated sense of awareness is your greatest tool, so know when you are most likely to fail and be extra prepared for specific things on specific days

You have to DECIDE.

You chose your habits. Then your habits become your behavior. This guide helps you ReBoot your Path of Wellness.

You CAN do it

Simply put, we are a collection of our decisions driven by our motivations... the things that we hold to be our beliefs and values. This is your moment to start controlling your decisions.

ReWire Your Thinking

Physical fitness and exercise is thrilling and invigorating on a daily basis. Once it is a part of your daily programming, you will appreciate it, but if you don't like the thought of exercise at this moment, this is your tool to ReWire and ReBoot.

EACH	DAY	YOU	CHOSE	YOUR	OWN	DECISIONS
					1 Today you will feel excited and motivated. Affirm Yourself!	2 Today you will still be excited and focused. Affirm Yourself!
3 SABOTAGE ALERT. Reaffirm Your WHY! This time is different!	4 SABOTAGE ALERT. Reaffirm yourself with pictures and quotes.	5 SABOTAGE ALERT. Reaffirm yourself with a positive mantra like "I AM THE BOSS!"	6 STAY ALERT TODAY	7 POSITIVE HABIT CREATION GOAL #1	8 STAY ALERT TODAY	9 STAY ALERT TODAY
10 SABOTAGE ALERT. Reaffirm Your WHY! This time is different!	11 SABOTAGE ALERT. Reaffirm yourself with pictures and quotes.	12 SABOTAGE ALERT. Reaffirm yourself with a positive mantra like "I AM FIT!"	13 STAY ALERT TODAY	14 POSITIVE HABIT CREATION GOAL #2	15 STAY ALERT TODAY	16 STAY ALERT TODAY
17 SABOTAGE ALERT. Reaffirm Your WHY! This time is different!	18 SABOTAGE ALERT. Reaffirm yourself with pictures and quotes.	19 SABOTAGE ALERT. Reaffirm yourself with a positive mantra like "I AM WORTHY!"	20 STAY ALERT TODAY	21 REWIRE GOAL #1. You DID IT!	22 STAY ALERT TODAY	23 BOOM! YOU DID IT. START OVER!

#Fitness4Ever Calendar

"REBOOT HABIT CALENDAR" by Coach Seay

2ND 23 DAYS

Changing Habits - Psychology

Science has shown us that if you can change a habit for 23 consecutive days, you can remap a NEGATIVE behavior to a desired behavior. Repeat the 23-day mental exercise for two additional periods of 23 days and you can close the door on going back to a bad habit or behavior. Self-Sabotage is important to avoid during a process of rewiring your choices and habits and an elevated sense of awareness is your greatest tool, so know when you are most likely to fail and be extra prepared for specific things on specific days

You have to DECIDE.

You chose your habits. Then your habits become your behavior. This guide helps you ReBoot your Path of Wellness.

You CAN do it

Simply put, we are a collection of our decisions driven by our motivations... the things that we hold to be our beliefs and values. This is your moment to start controlling your decisions.

ReWire Your Thinking

Physical fitness and exercise is thrilling and invigorating on a daily basis. Once it is a part of your daily programming, you will appreciate it, but if you don't like the thought of exercise at this moment, this is your tool to ReWire and ReBoot.

EACH	DAY	YOU	CHOSE	YOUR	OWN	DECISIONS
					1 Today you will feel excited and motivated. Affirm Yourself!	2 Today you will still be excited and focused. Affirm Yourself!
3 SABOTAGE ALERT. Reaffirm Your WHY! This time is different!	4 SABOTAGE ALERT. Reaffirm yourself with pictures and quotes.	5 SABOTAGE ALERT. Reaffirm yourself with a positive mantra like "I AM THE BOSS!"	6 STAY ALERT TODAY	7 POSITIVE HABIT CREATION GOAL #1	8 STAY ALERT TODAY	9 STAY ALERT TODAY
10 SABOTAGE ALERT. Reaffirm Your WHY! This time is different!	11 SABOTAGE ALERT. Reaffirm yourself with pictures and quotes.	12 SABOTAGE ALERT. Reaffirm yourself with a positive mantra like "I AM FIT!"	13 STAY ALERT TODAY	14 POSITIVE HABIT CREATION GOAL #2	15 STAY ALERT TODAY	16 STAY ALERT TODAY
17 SABOTAGE ALERT. Reaffirm Your WHY! This time is different!	18 SABOTAGE ALERT. Reaffirm yourself with pictures and quotes.	19 SABOTAGE ALERT. Reaffirm yourself with a positive mantra like "I AM WORTHY!"	20 STAY ALERT TODAY	21 REWIRE GOAL #1. You DID IT!	22 STAY ALERT TODAY	23 BOOM! YOU DID IT. START OVER!

#Fitness4Ever Calendar

"REBOOT HABIT CALENDAR" by Coach Seay

3RD 23 DAYS

Changing Habits - Psychology

Science has shown us that if you can change a habit for 23 consecutive days, you can remap a NEGATIVE behavior to a desired behavior. Repeat the 23-day mental exercise for two additional periods of 23 days and you can close the door on going back to a bad habit or behavior. Self-Sabotage is important to avoid during a process of rewiring your choices and habits and an elevated sense of awareness is your greatest tool, so know when you are most likely to fail and be extra prepared for specific things on specific days

You have to DECIDE.

You chose your habits. Then your habits become your behavior. This guide helps you ReBoot your Path of Wellness.

You CAN do it

Simply put, we are a collection of our decisions driven by our motivations... the things that we hold to be our beliefs and values. This is your moment to start controlling your decisions.

ReWire Your Thinking

Physical fitness and exercise is thrilling and invigorating on a daily basis. Once it is a part of your daily programming, you will appreciate it, but if you don't like the thought of exercise at this moment, this is your tool to ReWire and ReBoot.

EACH	DAY	YOU	CHOSE	YOUR	OWN	DECISIONS
					1 Today you will feel excited and motivated. Affirm Yourself!	2 Today you will still be excited and focused. Affirm Yourself!
3 SABOTAGE ALERT. Reaffirm Your WHY! This time is different!	4 SABOTAGE ALERT. Reaffirm yourself with pictures and quotes.	5 SABOTAGE ALERT. Reaffirm yourself with a positive mantra like "I AM THE BOSS!"	6 STAY ALERT TODAY	7 POSITIVE HABIT CREATION GOAL #1	8 STAY ALERT TODAY	9 STAY ALERT TODAY
10 SABOTAGE ALERT. Reaffirm Your WHY! This time is different!	11 SABOTAGE ALERT. Reaffirm yourself with pictures and quotes.	12 SABOTAGE ALERT. Reaffirm yourself with a positive mantra like "I AM FIT!"	13 STAY ALERT TODAY	14 POSITIVE HABIT CREATION GOAL #2	15 STAY ALERT TODAY	16 STAY ALERT TODAY
17 SABOTAGE ALERT. Reaffirm Your WHY! This time is different!	18 SABOTAGE ALERT. Reaffirm yourself with pictures and quotes.	19 SABOTAGE ALERT. Reaffirm yourself with a positive mantra like "I AM WORTHY!"	20 STAY ALERT TODAY	21 REWIRE GOAL #1. You DID IT!	22 STAY ALERT TODAY	23 BOOM! YOU DID IT. START OVER!

#Hustle4Ever

define your success

fingerprint

NOTES:

___

So you Instagram, eh???　　Follow me @Hustle4EverLife
Want to talk/text?　　　　　Chello me at 843-364-6720
Care to email?　　　　　　　david@seaydevelopment.com
Want me to Speak?　　　　　Chello me at 843-364-6720
Want to buy my book?　　　　Text me your email 843-364-6720

#Hustle4Ever ™ Fingerprint Series Notes. All Rights Reserved. Reproduce with Permission.

www.ingramcontent.com/pod-product-compliance
Lightning Source LLC
Chambersburg PA
CBHW070119110526
44587CB00015BA/2536